JULIO CORTÁZAR

In the same series:

LEONID ANDREYEV *Josephine M. Newcombe*
ISAAC BABEL *R. W. Hallett*
SAUL BELLOW *Brigitte Scheer-Schäzler*
BERTOLT BRECHT *Willy Haas*
ALBERT CAMUS *Carol Petersen*
WILLA CATHER *Dorothy Tuck McFarland*
COLETTE *Robert Cottrell*
JOHN DOS PASSOS *George J. Becker*
THEODORE DREISER *James Lundquist*
FRIEDRICH DÜRRENMATT *Armin Arnold*
T. S. ELIOT *Joachim Seyppel*
WILLIAM FAULKNER *Joachim Seyppel*
MAX FRISCH *Carol Petersen*
ROBERT FROST *Elaine Barry*
MAKSIM GORKI *Gerhard Habermann*
GÜNTER GRASS *Kurt Lothar Tank*
PETER HANDKE *Nicholas Hern*
ERNEST HEMINGWAY *Samuel Shaw*
HERMANN HESSE *Franz Baumer*
UWE JOHNSON *Mark Boulby*
JAMES JOYCE *Armin Arnold*
FRANZ KAFKA *Franz Baumer*
SINCLAIR LEWIS *James Lundquist*
GEORG LUKÁCS *Ehrhard Bahr and Ruth Goldschmidt Kunzer*
THOMAS MANN *Arnold Bauer*
ALBERTO MORAVIA *Jane E. Cottrell*
VLADIMIR NABOKOV *Donald E. Morton*
EUGENE O'NEILL *Horst Frenz*
JOSÉ ORTEGA Y GASSET *Franz Niedermayer*
GEORGE ORWELL *Roberta Kalechofsky*
KATHERINE ANNE PORTER *John Edward Hardy*
EZRA POUND *Jeannette Lander*
MARCEL PROUST *James R. Hewitt*
RAINER MARIA RILKE *Arnold Bauer*
JEAN-PAUL SARTRE *Liselotte Richter*
ISAAC BASHEVIS SINGER *Irving Malin*
THORNTON WILDER *Hermann Stresau*
THOMAS WOLFE *Fritz Heinrich Ryssel*
VIRGINIA WOOLF *Manly Johnson*
RICHARD WRIGHT *David Bakish*

Modern Literature Monographs

JULIO CORTÁZAR

Evelyn Picon Garfield

Frederick Ungar Publishing Co.
New York

Printed in the United States of America
Library of Congress Catalog Card Number: 74-78440
Designed by Anita Duncan
ISBN: 0-8044-2224-9

To my husband, Lou,
and my children, Audrey and Gene
—my three bridges to reality

Acknowledgments

I should like to thank Julio Cortázar and Ugné for their hospitality to me and my husband during our visit to Saignon. The interview was supported in part by a grant from the Penrose Fund of the American Philosophical Society. I should also like to express my gratitude to Irene Tractenberg for her editorial skill and kindred spirit and to Linda Levine for her encouragement.

For the convenience of the reader all Spanish titles are also given in English. Published translations are distinguished from literal translations by the use of italics or quotes, depending on the genre. Whenever an English translation exists and is noted in the bibliography, that translation has been used as a source of citations. Otherwise the citation translations are those of the author of this book.

Contents

Chronology

1914: 26 August: Julio Cortázar is born in Brussels, Belgium of Argentinean parents.

1918: Returns to Argentina to live in Banfield, a suburb of Buenos Aires.

1932: Earns a degree as an elementary school teacher.

1935: Earns a degree as a secondary and preparatory school teacher.

1936: Passes first year examinations at the university.

1937–44: Leaves studies to work as a high school teacher in Bolívar and Chivilcoy. Starts to write short stories.

1938: Publishes *Presencia* (Presence), a collection of poems, and signs it with the pseudonym Julio Denís.

1944–45: Teaches courses in French literature at the University of Cuyo. Participates in the occupation of the university in protest against Peronism. Is arrested but freed shortly afterwards. Renounces his post.

1946–48: Moves to Buenos Aires where he works as the manager of the Argentine Publishing Association (Cámara Argentina del Libro). Earns a degree as a public translator after passing examinations in languages and law.

1948–51: Leaves the managerial position to begin work as a public translator.

1949: Publishes a dramatic poem, *Los reyes* (The Kings), using his own name for the first time.

1951: Is awarded a scholarship by the French government to study in Paris. Leaves Argentina the same month in which his first collection of short stories, *Bestiario* (Bestiary), is published.

1952: Remains in Paris and begins work as a freelance translator for UNESCO.

1953: Marries Aurora Bernárdez, an Argentinean and a translator. Visits Italy where he translates the prose works of Edgar Allan Poe for the University of Puerto Rico. Writes much of *Historias de cronopios y de famas* (*Cronopios and Famas*).

1956: Publishes the short story collection *Final del juego* (*End of the Game and Other Stories*) and *Obras en prosa* (Prose Works of Edgar Allan Poe).

1958: Publishes the short story collection *Las armas secretas* (Secret Weapons).

1960: Publishes his first novel *Los premios* (*The Winners*). Visits the United States, in particular Washington, D.C., and Greenwich Village in New York.

1962: Publishes the anecdotes of *Historias de cronopios y de famas (Cronopios and Famas).*

1963: Publishes the novel *Rayuela* (*Hopscotch*). Makes first visit to post-revolutionary Cuba.

1965: *The Winners* is published in English translation by Pantheon in the United States.

1966: Publishes the short story collection *Todos los fuegos el fuego* (*All Fires The Fire*). *Hopscotch* is published in English translation by Pantheon in the United States.

1967: Publishes his first collage-book, *La vuelta al día en ochenta mundos* (Around the Day in Eighty Worlds). *Blow-Up and Other Stories* is published in English translation by Pantheon in the United States. Previously in hard cover edition under the title *End of the Game and Other Stories.*

1968: Publishes the novel *62: Modelo para armar* (*62: A Model Kit*).

1969: Publishes his second collage-book *Ultimo Round* (Last Round). *Cronopios and Famas* is published in English translation by Pantheon in the United States.

1970: Publishes *Viaje alrededor de una mesa* (A Trip Around the Table).

1971: Publishes *Pameos y Meopas* (Pameos and Meopas), a collection of poems.

1972: Publishes *Prosa del observatorio* (Prose from the Observatory). *62: A Model Kit* is published in English translation by Pantheon in the United States.

1973: Travels to Argentina to commemorate the publication of his novel *Libro de Manuel* (Book of Manuel). Also visits Peru, Ecuador and Chile. *All Fires The Fire* is published in English translation by Pantheon in the United States.

An Encounter With Julio Cortázar

The snail lives the way I like to live.
He carries his own house with him.
—*Julio Cortázar*

On Monday, July 9, 1973, at 4:00 in the afternoon, a heavily bearded and long-haired Julio Cortázar waited for me on the platform of the train station in Avignon, France. It was not difficult to single him out since with a height of 6 feet 6 inches his imposing figure clad in dungarees, a brown shirt and sunglasses towered above the crowd. He had just returned from an unexpected UNESCO conference on the Impact of Science and Technology on Modern Society. He was a consultant for the first time, since he is usually a free-lance interpreter for that organization in Paris. We drove in his VW camper bus through the countryside of southern France to the small village of Saignon where Cortázar lives from May to September.

There in Saignon, atop a hill overlooking what he calls "his" valleys of vineyards and fields of lavender, Cortázar's home is perched in a solitary niche on the slopes of the village. The swallows darted through the air and the frogs croaked to what seemed like a perfect time schedule. Breaking the tranquil silence was almost treasonous.

He bought his summer home eight years ago in the High Provence because of the view and the solitude. The house of plaster and stone masonry with the typical orange tile roof of the region was originally a small shepherd's shelter, he explained. That shelter is now the "*cave*" or pantry onto which several other rooms were built when Cortázar purchased the house. Nevertheless the wooden beamed interior has taken on the shape and tastes of this tall Argentinean. A large modern living room with a vaulted ceiling, and a fireplace and a study with a loft have been added. The kitchen floor had to be dropped and the second floor bedroom ceiling raised to accommodate Cortázar's height.

The rooms are filled with paintings and posters of some of his favorite artists, the Argentinean Julio Silva and the Rumanian surrealist Victor Brauner. Here and there on the walls and shelves are surrealist objects of his own invention—a small box containing compartments filled with painted pebbles, snail shells and bits of broken mirrors guarded by a tiny red gate with a compass as a knob and a box with an egg carton containing a protruding candle alongside of a picture of a phallus discreetly covered with a plastic bag and criss-crossed strings. A guitar given to him by the Chilean poet Pablo Neruda stands in the corner of the living room.

We sat in the living room and talked of his life and works. Cortázar, comfortable in shorts, usually sipped a cold drink and smoked a Dutch cigar or a pipe. His enormous eyes periodically flashed but constantly eluded precise chromatic definition—sometimes green or blue or gray. They seemed to echo a grin that bared two widely separated front teeth. That mischievous smile, I thought, belonged to a man who in less than two months, on August 26th, would be fifty-nine years old.

When he spoke in his resonant voice, he frequently tapped his foot softly and almost imperceptibly as if keeping time to the rhythm of his words. Cortázar's Argentinean Spanish contains a noticeably guttural French "r" which is not a result of his residence in

France since 1951. Instead, he explained, it is due to the fact that he was born in Brussels, Belgium, of Argentine parents abroad on business. His father's great grandparents were from the Basque Province of Spain; his mother's family can be traced back to France and Germany. Cortázar and his parents did not return to Banfield, a suburb of Buenos Aires, until he was four years old. By that time he had already acquired the French "r" and was never to lose it.

In Argentina Cortázar was raised by his mother and aunt for when he was a small child his father abandoned the family. As a young boy he was interested in fantastic literature. He recalled that his friends would return unread books he had lent them: they were bored with his favorite magical authors. At the age of ten he wanted to be a sailor: "Since I was little, and I think it was Jules Verne's fault, travel was the ultimate purpose in life for me." However, travel was an expensive undertaking in Argentina and he was a sickly child. Instead, Cortázar became a public school teacher and left his university studies in order to help the financial situation at home.

In 1944, he was invited to give courses in French literature at the University of Cuyo. One year later he abandoned his post there in protest against Peronism. After returning to Buenos Aires he assumed the position of director of a publishing association and later studied for a year to earn a degree in public translating—a profession requiring knowledge in languages and law. In 1951, however, he received a scholarship from the French government to study in France. It was in Paris the following year that he began a career as a free-lance translator for UNESCO. He had already published a dramatic poem, *Los reyes* (The Kings), and a collection of short stories, *Bestiario* (Bestiary).

Except for periodic visits to Argentina and other countries, Cortázar has lived in France for more than twenty years. Many Latin Americans criticize his residence abroad. In answer to them Cortázar replied: "I cannot deny an inclination that perhaps began due to my being born in Belgium and to my having spoken French in my early childhood; it is a profound contact with the culture and the spiritual values of France." By reading Cortázar's words or by listening to his Argentinean intonation, one can readily perceive that he has not turned his back on his native land. As he affirms: "Actually I am not Frenchified. Simultaneously, I am the most Argentinean of Argentineans. There is a very French Cortázar and another, who is profoundly Argentinean. And they are perfectly separated." In fact, Cortázar carries Argentina with him wherever he goes, somewhat like a snail, an animal dear to him which appears frequently in his works: "I think that that's what I like about the snail. The fact that he doesn't have to return like a spider or other insects to his nest. He carries his nest with him and travels all over the world."

During the rest of the year, Cortázar resides in a small apartment in the Latin Quarter of Paris near Notre Dame. It is somewhat uncomfortable, he commented, for the ceilings are too low; but everything he likes is nearby—movies, cafes, the Seine. "Paris and I have an amorous relationship," he told me. He loves wandering through the streets, attending the theater, concerts, and art expositions, and visiting friends. Cortázar has applied for French citizenship since he is tired of being a foreigner in France. He would like to participate as a responsible citizen. However, he was quick to remind me that he would never have requested French papers if he had to give up his Argentinean citizenship.

Cortázar considers himself an international writer. "I am absolutely the opposite of the kind of writer, above all the Latin American author, who likes to stay in his own country and in his own corner and who writes about what's around him." Cortázar's fiction is universal in its appeal because it reflects every man's search for himself and for a world to his liking; it discovers the fantastic elements of life born of daily reality; and it is always innovative and imaginative. Cortázar seldom forgets that man has a humorous facet, a playfulness which is often his salvation. "It would be absolutely impossible for me to live if I couldn't play." By play, Cortázar means the right to listen to music, to paint, to take a walk if he feels like doing so. "That's the meaning of play: everything that doesn't represent work, obligation and moral necessity."

Seen from the historical perspective of Argentinean literature, Julio Cortázar envisions himself as the only one of his generation to partake of the two schools of Argentinean writing of that period: the Jorge Luis Borges' tendency toward hyper-intellectualism, rigorous prose, and universality and the Roberto Arlt approach toward sensuous, erotic, earthy city atmospheres expressed in an unkempt language. From Borges, Cortázar recalled, he learned to be ethically implacable with himself as a writer. From Arlt, Cortázar could sense an enormously intuitive creative force.

Cortázar asserted that he also writes intuitively

and from actual experience, conscious or subconscious. "I don't think I've ever written anything intellectual." He even contended that the philosophical conversations in his novel *Rayuela* (*Hopscotch*) were secondary to the theme and to the intuitions developed there.

Julio Cortázar is individualistic in his literary preferences. His library is composed of French—the majority—and English books. Only a small portion of his volumes are in Spanish. Since youth he has enjoyed English poetry in particular—the romantics, Shakespeare, and especially Keats. "For me English is the language of poetry." He cited Rainer Maria Rilke as a strong poetic influence on him. "I read a lot of poetry. No one asks me or interviews me about poetic themes. Nevertheless poetry is absolutely necessary to me. And if I have some sort of regret it is that my work is definitely not an exclusively poetic work. I think that part of my prose is thought of, seen and written poetically."

In his youth he was so strongly influenced by French Surrealism that even today, in a letter to me, he recognized its impact on his writings: "Even though the presence of Surrealism is perhaps not as 'all pervading' as you think, it undeniably constituted the most intensive motivating force of all or nearly all of my books, something which can't please me enough."

During the interview, Cortázar often referred to the importance of critics in influencing and interpreting his works.

I never register influences consciously. In my case, the critics must point them out . . . I learn a lot about myself. Because actually there are many interpretations that I believe to be either completely or partially accurate. Thus they show me pieces of my own mosaic, or my unknown unconscious. They show me my nocturnal self, nocturnal in the psychological sense, and in that sense I'm very grateful for that kind of interpretation.

Though in the last few years Cortázar has been particularly fascinated by books on psychology, psychoanalysis and anthropology, he noted that much of the Latin American fiction published in the last ten years is excellent and has had international repercussions. He cited Mario Vargas Llosa's *La ciudad y los perros* (*The Time of the Hero*) for its technical innovations, Gabriel García Marquez's *Cien años de soledad* (*One Hundred Years of Solitude*) for its "miraculous torrent of fabulous invention," and Carlos Fuentes's *Aura*, noting that he would have liked to have written the latter himself. "I envy him a lot for that story." Internationally disposed in his reading preferences, however, he confessed his recent fascination with the genius of John Barth's *Lost in the Funhouse.*

Julio Cortázar places great importance on individuality in sports, music, and politics, all of which play an important role in his life and works. Many times during our conversations he demonstrated a preference for the individual rather than the group. In sports he favored boxing or tennis to team sports. He called it "individual destinies that play themselves out one against the other." In classical music, along with Wagner and Italian opera, he preferred chamber music to orchestras. He described jazz as "the only surrealistic music" and has been an ardent fan since 1925. As an amateur jazz musician, he chose the trumpet because he felt it to be the most erotic musical instrument. In jazz, too, he generally disliked the big band sounds, with the exception of Duke Ellington, preferring small groups where the individual's brilliance is exhibited.

Although he firmly believes in the advent of socialism as the destiny of Latin America, he conceives of socialist man as an individual who should not have to give up his liberties: "My idea of socialist man is a man in a more just society where no one is exploited or is an exploiter, but a man who doesn't lose any of his individual capabilities. And up to now, no society has achieved that."

Five days of conversations with Julio Cortázar is a truly unique experience. It is a collage of images—Charlie Parker records, a visit to the remains of the Marquis de Sade's castle in nearby Lacoste, a pine tree planted by Cortázar in the garden six years ago under the eyes of incredulous farmers who said it would never grow, Joni Mitchell's "Ladies of the Canyon," Gorgonzola cheese, verses of songs like "Old rocking chair's got me," and wondering why his newly adopted cat Demosthenes was still not home. In fact, Julio Cortázar is a collage-personality.

1

A Swiss Cheese Reality

I'm the first one to be surprised by the endings of almost all my short stories.
—Julio Cortázar

In 1962, after having written four of his five collections of short stories, Julio Cortázar published an article entitled "Algunos aspectos del cuento" (Some Aspects of the Short Story).[1] Designating the short story as "a mysterious brother to poetry in another dimension of literary time," Cortázar defined the omnipresent element of fantasy in his short stories as the result of a desire to express the illogical exceptions and not the rational rules that govern our lives.

> Almost all the short stories that I have written belong to the genre called "fantastic" for lack of a better name, and they oppose that false realism that consists of believing that all things can be described and explained according to the philosophical and scientific optimism of the eighteenth century, that is, as part of a world ruled more or less harmoniously by a system of laws of principles, of cause and effect relationships or defined psychologies, of well mapped geographies. In my case, the suspicion of another more secret and less communicable order, and the rich discovery of Alfred Jarry, for whom the true study of reality did not reside in laws but in exceptions to the laws, have been some of the principles which oriented me in my personal search for a literature on the outskirts of a realism that is far too ingenuous.

The fantastic for Cortázar is a momentary alteration in the laws or rational order of reality. The exception, however, must become accepted as if it were the rule without entirely displacing the traditional order into which it has ingressed. The exceptional or fantastic in his short stories, therefore, coexists with our conventional world. Thus its presence is even more disturbing and provocative. The fantastic in Cortázar's short stories does not always "take over" or usurp logical reality, instead it infiltrates and subverts it. "The fantastic is born of a very real situation," he explained during our interview.

In the same article, Cortázar drew an interesting parallel between the novel as movie and the short story as photograph. A movie has an open order, a detailed and rounded structure in which many frames or puzzle pieces eventually deliver a finished story to the viewer, as in a novel. A photograph, on the other hand, presupposes limitations. It is one immobile frame, a single significant piece to a puzzle, a fragment of reality to which the viewer must supply the remaining pieces, as in a short story.

The short story, therefore, is an "opening up" onto a reality that is much greater than that of the actual tale: "that fabulous opening of the minute onto the gigantic, of that which is individual and circumscribed onto the very essence of the human condition."

Cortázar maintains that although the writer often chooses a theme for a short story, many times the theme imposes itself upon him, pushing him to write it: "In my case, the great majority of my short stories were written—how shall I say—almost involuntarily, without the approval of a reasoned consciousness, as if I were only a medium through whom a strange force passed and manifested itself." He maintained during the interview that he has always been ashamed to sign his short stories because he feels that he actually doesn't write them; they come to him, he finds them and records them.

In another essay entitled "Del cuento breve y sus alrededores" (The Short Story and Its Surroundings), which appeared in 1969 in his book *Ultimo Round* (Last Round), Cortázar described the short story as exorcism. To explain the cathartic effect of expressing a theme which has imposed itself on him, he cited a verse by Chile's Nobel Prize poet, Pablo Neruda: "My creatures are born of a long rejection." Often plagued by the need to unburden himself of his thoughts and feelings, Cortázar finds himself seized by a great intensity that he likens to Poe's "state of trance."

To Cortázar the experience of reading a short story should be similar to that of writing it. In this way the reader partakes of the author's personal creation. The internal tension of the author, present in the short story, must fascinate the reader and cause him to lose contact with the reality that surrounds him. It must immerse him in the short story so that he emerges from the reading—much as the author had from the writing —"as if from an act of love, exhausted and oblivious to the surrounding world, to which he returns little by little with a surprised look of slow recognition, many times of relief and other times of resignation."

For Cortázar a short story is born without thought like an "enormous clot" wrenched from the subconscious. It surfaces to jar his daily life. In the same essay he describes his own circumstance as a short story writer:

> . . . I see a man relatively happy and mundane, wrapped up in the same trivialities and dentists as any inhabitant of a great city, who reads the newspaper, falls in love and goes to the theater and who, all of a sudden, instantaneously, on a subway ride, in a café, in a dream, in the office while

revising a suspicious looking translation about illiteracy in Tanzania, stops being man-and-his-circumstance and for no *reason* at all, without warning, without an epileptic air, without the contraction that precedes a bad headache, without anything that gives you time to grit your teeth and breathe deeply, *it is a short story*, a shapeless mass without words or faces or beginning or end but already a short story, something that can only be a short story and besides at once, immediately, Tanzania can go to Hell because this man will put a piece of paper in the typewriter and will start to write even though his bosses and the United Nations are breathing down his neck, even though his wife calls him because the soup is getting cold, even though great things are happening in the world and he ought to listen to the news on the radio or take a bath or telephone some friends.

That's a pretty interpretation; it's not mine
but it could be. Why not?
—*Julio Cortázar*

Bestiario (Bestiary)

"In some ways writing is like an exorcism, a rejection of invading creatures by projecting them into a state that paradoxically gives them universal existence and at the same time places them at the end of a bridge far from where the narrator stands . . ." These words by Julio Cortázar in one of his recent books, *Ultimo Round*, are particularly applicable to his first collection of short stories, *Bestiario*, 1951. The title alludes to the invading creatures, imaginary and real, which inhabit the stories as well as his mind. They symbolize repressed instincts, phobias, and obsessions that from time to time invade his consciousness.

These stories, written from 1945 to 1950 have one important literary precursor, *Los reyes*, 1949 (The Kings), which Cortázar refers to as his "dramatic poem." Although written in a lofty and highly polished style, atypical of his other works, *Los reyes* is one of Cortázar's favorites. It is easy to see why, for it is a thematic cornerstone of his literary career. In the original Greek myth, upon which it is based, Minos, king of Crete, promises to sacrifice to the gods a white bull sent to him by Neptune. When he tricks the gods by sacrificing another bull in its place, Neptune angrily seeks revenge by compelling Minos's wife Pasiphaë to fall in love with the animal. The Minotaur, half bull and half man, is born of the union. Minos imprisons the Minotaur in a labyrinth and offers him the sacrifice of seven men and seven women every nine years. When one of the sacrificial victims, Theseus, arrives, Ariadne, the daughter of Minos and Pasiphaë, falls in love with him. She provides him with a sword and a thread before entering the labyrinth. With them he winds his way into the maze, kills the beast, and is able to find his way out again. In the traditional legend, we see that the Minotaur is the monster to be killed by the hero Theseus with the help of Ariadne.

Julio Cortázar's approach to the classic myth is quite different; it is a defense of the Minotaur. For him the beast is symbolic of a free spirit who is locked up because he is different. Contrary to the myth, Ariadne is in love with him—he is her half brother for they are both Pasiphaë's offspring. Ariadne gives the thread to

Theseus, not so that he can find his way out again but so that the Minotaur can kill him and then wind *his* way through the labyrinth to freedom and her. In Cortázar's version, the Minotaur is to be the hero.

Even though Cortázar's *Los reyes* was hardly noticed, this does not diminish its importance; in it Cortázar interprets the classical myth from a new perspective that uncovers a hidden facet of reality beneath the traditionally accepted one. The Minotaur can be seen as a symbol of man's suppressed instincts, locked up yet nurtured, of the sometimes horrifying "other" in our dreams, and of the nonconformity met with disapproving and hostile eyes by society at large. Ariadne had not only accepted the beast but had tried to free him from his prison. Before dying, the Minotaur sensed his importance to her and promised to live on as instinct and dream not only in her memory but also in the collective subconscious of mankind, irritating and provoking humanity. In *Bestiario*, Cortázar reincarnates the Minotaur.

In an interview with the critic Luis Harss, the author commented on the importance of the stories collected in *Bestiario*: "They were glimpses, dimensions, or hints of possibilities that terrified or fascinated me and that I had to exhaust by working them off in the story."[2] Therefore, he accepts the creatures stalking his mind, at times even sympathizes with them, as do the characters in his stories who accept their own monsters. These characters are usually common people: a wealthy brother and sister, a translator, a bank employee, a nurse, a merchant, an adolescent girl. In many stories, the streets and districts of Buenos Aires are mentioned to substantiate the concrete world in which the characters live. The settings (houses, apartments, dance halls) and the daily routines (knitting, caring for and raising animals, playing games) are described in minute detail in order to impress the reader with the normalcy of the atmosphere in which the characters move. When Cortázar has won the reader's confidence, he proceeds to subvert the banal reality and to sabotage the established order of their lives as we see in "Casa tomada" ("The House Taken Over").

This story, which first appeared in a periodical, *Los Anales de Buenos Aires* (1946), installs the reader in the daily world of an elderly and well-to-do brother and sister who while away the hours cleaning a large house, cooking, collecting stamps, and knitting. Irene and her brother, who remains nameless, live in a part of the house that is partitioned off from the other section by a massive oak door. One day, while preparing *mate* in the kitchen, the brother hears a muted sound on the other side of the door, like "a chair being knocked over onto the carpet or the muffled buzzing of conversation." He bolts the door closed and returns to Irene. "I had to shut the door to the passage. They've taken over the back part." Without surprise or anxiety they decide quite simply to carry on as usual on the safe side of the door, although several of their prized possessions remained in the "part taken over." They settle down to a slightly altered life until once again the noise invades the house on *their* side of the oak door in the kitchen. They run out into the street, dropping everything, locking the door and tossing the key down the sewer. Irene's skein of knitting wool traces their flight from the house, for it unwinds as they escape and now leads from the street under the front door back into the "house taken over," like an Ariadne's thread in search of another mysterious Minotaur.

"Casa tomada" has been interpreted in various ways: as a symbol of the socio-political reality of a new generation replacing an old wealthy one in the wake of the dictator Perón in Argentina; as the obsessive presence of the ancestors condemning the incestuous relationship; and as the mind besieged by mysterious, unknown forces, accepted as reality, that prevent one from leading a calm, everyday life. Cortázar, however, related the genesis of this story to me.

"It is actually a story that for me has absolutely no other meaning than that of a nightmare. That doesn't prevent one from analyzing the nightmare." He had dreamt that he was alone in a house full of passageways when suddenly he heard a noise from the depths of the corridor. He had a sensation of nightmarish terror. After quickly closing the door and bolting it tight, for a few minutes he felt safe and thought that the nightmare would become a peaceful dream. All of a sudden the noise sounded on his side of the door. He woke up, and still in his pajamas, without taking time to brush his teeth or comb his hair, he sat down at the typewriter. In about an hour and a half "The House Taken Over" was written.

The mind as a house infested with unknown invaders is also interestingly portrayed in "Cefalea," a story suggested to Cortázar by an article about homeopathy, the system of curing diseases by administering medicine to produce desired symptoms. In "Cefalea" the characters raise strange animals called "mancuspias," and suffer symptoms of an illness that seems to worsen as the howling animals, escaping from their cages, circle the house. The "mancuspias" begin to die, and aggravated symptoms augur the death of the custodians as well. Whereas in "Casa tomada," Cortázar depicts a strange invasion of the house manifest to the reader and the characters only as an unidentifiable noise, in "Cefalea" the unknown materializes into fantastic creatures. Cortázar deliberately describes the animals and the symptoms suffered by their custodians in pseudoscientific terms. This technique causes the reader to view the eerie physical invasion of the house by the escaped animals as a symbolic rendering of the mind psychologically inhabited by creatures. Cortázar explains that ever since youth he has suffered from severe migraine headaches, and that in "Cefalea" he transformed the sensations he periodically experiences from them into a short story dealing with the fantastic.

Similarly, the fantastic coexists with the real in the title story, "Bestiario." This anecdote also originates in a dream that Cortázar had. When he was ill with a fever, in an almost delirious state he pictured a house in which a live tiger threateningly roamed the rooms. But the tiger was controlled in some way by the people who lived in the house. "Of course, that tiger was my fever to some extent, my hallucination," he assured me.

In "Bestiario" a young girl, Isabel, visits her relatives, the Funes family. Rema and Luis, their little boy Nino and Luis' brother, the Kid, live in a house besieged by a tiger. The animal roams the maze of rooms, tacitly regulating the lives of the inhabitants who accept its presence. Isabel adheres to the warnings used by the Funes family to prevent running into the tiger in the house. Through letters from Isabel to her mother, we sense an intimacy between her Aunt Rema and the young girl and an aversion of the two toward Rema's brother-in-law, the Kid. Amidst the growing tension, Isabel seizes the opportunity to misinform the Kid of the tiger's whereabouts. As she hides her face in her aunt's lap, Isabel hears his dying screams, muffled by Rema's skirt. The tiger as a menacing force in the house seems to echo the cruelty of the Kid toward Rema and at the same time symbolizes Isabel's hidden desire and mechanism for disposing of her threatening uncle.

This short but intense story employs several effective techniques that are to be found in Cortázar's later works. With Isabel, he masters the sympathetic portrayal of the adolescent mind in its emotional ambiguity. His descriptions, which excel in sensual imagery, at times acquire a hallucinatory air as if in a Salvador Dalí painting or a Luis Buñuel film. In "Bestiario," Isabel's cousin and playmate Nino has an ant farm in his room. At one point in the story, when Aunt Rema appears at the doorway, her hand is reflected in the glass of the ant farm. The sight of her hand, which seems to crawl with ants, leads Isabel to associate the repulsive image with the odious Kid squeezing Rema's fingers as she served him coffee. This scene, with its provocative horror both to the reader and to Isabel, could easily recall a similar episode in Buñuel's film *Le chien andalou* of a hand crawling with ants.

When I asked Cortázar about his fascination with ants since they appear frequently in his fiction, he described a strange feeling of horror and attraction to the insect world. He recalled that at the age of seven he had a cat named Pituco. One morning he awoke to find the cat dead. Somehow it had eaten poison set out for the ants in the kitchen. He buried the cat in his own garden. The experience was his first encounter with death. Perhaps it is as a subconscious result of his experience that ants implacably find their way into the fascinating yet terrifying imagery in "Bestiario."

In that same short story Cortázar also succeeds in flashing reality before our eyes in film-like frames. The fleeting events and snatches of conversation are juxtaposed as in a collage of immediate, elliptical experience:

> "I don't like the idea either," her mother said, and Isabel knew, as if she were on a toboggan, that they were going to send her to the Funes home for the summer. . . . She felt afraid, delighted, smell of the willow trees and the *u* in the Funes was getting mixed in with the rice pudding, so late to be still up, and get up to bed, right now.[3]

This passage approximates the anxiety of Isabel's thought process as she experiences events beyond her control.

Some of the stories in *Bestiario* owe their genesis to Cortázar's need to handle feelings beyond his control, exorcising them by writing about them in a short story. As he explained in an essay in *Ultimo Round*, the stories "Carta a una señorita en París" ("Letter to a Young Lady in Paris") and "Circe" were closely related to mental therapy for him:

> Perhaps it is an exaggeration to state that all successful short stories, and especially the fantastic ones, are neurotic products, nightmares, or hallucinations which are neutralized as they materialize into concrete forms and are removed from the original seat of the neurosis; . . . in any case, in any memorable short story this polarity can be seen, as if the author had wanted to rid himself of the creature as quickly and as completely as possible, exorcising it in the only way possible for him: writing it.[4]

Cortázar has alluded to a time of unusual stress in Buenos Aires, when in hope of becoming financially independent he studied to become a public translator. While preparing for exams he began to develop neurotic symptoms. One of these, a recurring nausea, he described in "Carta a una señorita en París." In that story a translator moves into a friend's apartment, as Cortázar himself had done, while she is away in Paris. He finds that almost every time he rides up in the elevator, between the second and the third floor, he vomits up a live rabbit. This is not unusual since it happened to him before moving to her apartment. Neither is it repulsive to the reader, for the births are described in endearing terms:

> When I feel that I'm going to bring up a rabbit, I put two fingers in my mouth like an open pincer, and I wait to feel the lukewarm fluff rise in my throat like an effervescence in a sal hepatica. It's all swift and clean, passes in the briefest instant. I remove the fingers from my mouth and in them, held fast by the ears, is a small white rabbit. The bunny appears to be content, a perfectly normal bunny, only very tiny, small as a chocolate rabbit, only it's white and very thoroughly a rabbit.[5]

The first birth in the elevator is not too disturbing to the man, even though he does consider killing the rabbit. His anxiety increases, however, when he realizes that the rabbits will have to live with him in Andrea's apartment where they may destroy the "refined and compact order" of his friend's home. He is also further alarmed by the fact that the births begin to occur at more frequent intervals than before he had moved. The protagonist cares for the rabbits, hides them from the maid by day in the wardrobe, feeds them clover by night, and writes to Andrea in Paris. As they mature, however, the rabbits, created and nurtured by the man, begin to destroy the apartment, breaking lamps, chewing books, and staining rugs. The exhausted translator hopes in vain that he will bear no more rabbits.

In the last entry he makes to the letter which he has been writing to Andrea, after the birth of the eleventh rabbit, the despondent but resigned narrator realizes that the creatures—at once beautiful and terrifying—will continue to dominate his waking hours. He describes them amid the ruins of the apartment, as if in a rite worshiping their creator, "in a circle under the light of the lamp, in a circle as though they were adoring me, and suddenly they were yipping, they were crying like I never believed rabbits could cry." He subsequently suggests that at dawn no one will even notice the small rabbits splattered on the sidewalk below the balcony, for they will be too busy cleaning up the "other body" before the students pass by on their way to school. Although the protagonist in the story succumbs to his self-created and self-destructive creatures, it is obvious that the author has been relieved by exorcising his nausea in the short story.

In the same interview Cortázar explained that he wrote "Circe" under similar circumstances, in an effort to purge the fear of finding bugs or flies in his food. In a modern version of a Greek myth the enchantress Circe—who was adept at the art of concocting poisons, of making men ill in body and mind, and of transforming them into pigs—is reincarnated as Delia Mañara. Her name suggests the Spanish word "maraña," a thicket, maze or plot. She is courted by Mario, who ignores the rumors that the girl had killed her two boyfriends.

Delia mysteriously bewitches a cat as well as her boyfriends. One suitor, Hector, gives her a white rabbit, which dies shortly before he commits suicide. The story exudes a horror reminiscent of Edgar Allan Poe. It abounds in repulsive images: a fish's eye "like a living pearl . . . like a tear that would slide between the teeth while you chew it"; and Delia's home-made candy, "like a small rat between Delia's fingers, a tiny thing but alive." Mario, however, escapes her attempt to poison him, for when he squeezes open a bonbon, he discovers the white body of a cockroach amid crushed wings, bits of legs, marzipan, and mint.

Thus we see how Cortázar dwells on the surfacing of unknown forces within himself, nightmares, irrational phobias or instincts that he embodies in concrete forms in order to smoke out the devils that beset his mind. But man can be threatened by external forces as well.

Malevolence and humanity's bestiality manifest themselves more subtly and collectively in another story, "Omnibus." The nurse Clara boards a bus. (It is the same bus that Cortázar used to take to work every day in Buenos Aires.) In the story, Clara is not only attacked visually by the hostile glances of the other passengers, all of whom carry flowers, but also by the conductor who lunges toward her several times without successful contact. Only one young man, also "flowerless," who boards the bus after her, sympathizes silently with Clara. The bus careens down the streets, becoming as threateningly dangerous in its reckless speed as the aggressive people riding inside with Clara. It halts abruptly to drop the passengers off at the cemetery. At the last stop, Clara and the young man barely escape from the approaching and hostile conductor through the slamming doors into the plaza. There they immediately buy some pansies. In this way, they can be like the other passengers carrying their bouquets; like the Minotaur, they had been nonconformists, and had therefore been ostracized.

Like Clara, the reader begins to wonder if she and the young man are the only living passengers on the bus. Perhaps the others carrying flowers to the cemetery, are going to their own graves. Here, however, as in other stories by Cortázar, there are multiple levels of interpretation. An answer is not as important as the provocative uneasiness that the story creates in the reader. And that's exactly what Cortázar seems to want: to jar us out of our self-sufficient, complacent reality.

The two main characters of "Omnibus" want to escape *from* a nightmarish world. Conversely in "Las puertas del cielo" ("The Gates of Heaven") and "Lejana" ("The Distances"), the protagonists are mysteriously drawn *into* a dream reality that they cannot understand but feel compelled to experience. In these two stories, Julio Cortázar exposes his characters to the other side of visible reality where desire and hallucinations are materialized for them. Many of his characters search for a more desirable although elusive facet of reality. For instance, in "The Gates of Heaven," Marcelo and Mauro briefly glimpse Mauro's dead wife, Celina, among the couples at her old hangout, a dance hall. In death, she returns to the world from which Mauro had taken her, "her paradise finally gained." Marcelo watches a disbelieving Mauro stagger across the dance floor after her, trying to find "the gates of heaven among all that smoke and all those people."

The desire—in Mauro's case the futile attempt to see his dead wife Celina—to penetrate another side of reality materializes in the short story "Lejana." In that story Cortázar sketched themes of prime importance for future works: the participation of man in a world of his mind's creation; the experience of "otherness"; and the existence of magnetic fields, or "figures" as Cortázar calls them, that allow people to communicate with each other across time and space.

In "Lejana" the road to the oneiric zone opens with a simple word game of anagrams, described by Alina Reyes, the protagonist-narrator, in her diary: "Alina Reyes *es la reina y* . . . That one's so nice because it opens a path, because it does not close. Because the queen and . . . *la reina y* . . ."* Games play an important role in Cortázar's fiction, acquiring the power and function of rites of passage to the "sacred zone" of authentic reality lying hidden beneath the surface of daily existence.

During our interview Cortázar alluded to the year when he wrote "The Distances," noting that he had been impressed by the surrealist word games. That interest was compounded by a fascination with texts from the cabala. As a child he enjoyed reading words in reverse order, and as a young man he even collected and exchanged palindromes and anagrams with a friend who was a professor also.

In "Lejana" it is by means of such a word game

* "es la reina y" means "is the queen and . . ."

that Alina Reyes, a young woman living in Buenos Aires, becomes obsessed with a recurrent vision of a beggar woman in Budapest. Alina experiences the beggar's hardships especially during moments when she herself should be happy. Increasingly the illusion becomes a part of her reality. She writes: "There (I dreamed it, it's only a dream, but . . . it sticks and works itself into my wakefulness) . . ." Alina is tormented by the beatings she feels that the woman in Budapest is receiving. She experiences the cold, wet snow of Budapest entering her shoes as it likewise enters those of the beggar woman. Still she desires to meet her, to understand her. She is convinced that she, as the "queen" in the anagram, will save the beggar woman from her misery: "If I am really I, she will yield, she will join my radiant *zone*, my lovelier and surer life; I have only to go to her side and lay a hand on her shoulder."

Here the diary ends as Alina travels to Budapest on her honeymoon, and an omniscient author relates the meeting on the bridge between the two women, the embrace, the "total fusion." For, true to Alina's dream, which she not only chose to ignore but to challenge with delusions of being victorious, the beggar envelops Alina into her own zone of misery and changes places to enter into Alina's body. Alina becomes part of the other woman and watches through the beggar's eyes as the shell of her former self departs:

> Now she did scream. From the cold, because the snow was coming in through her broken shoes, because making her way along the roadway to the plaza went Alina Reyes, very lovely in her gray suit, her hair a little loose against the wind, not turning her face. Going off.[6]

The two women are "figures" in the same constellation. Their paths crossed, first through dreams provoked by a chance game, then by an intense sympathetic communication across time and space, and finally in an ecstasy of psychic exchange with one another.

The act of experiencing another's life, of the transmigration of one living being into another's body, is a theme in other stories by Cortázar, such as "Axolotl" and "La noche boca arriba" ("The Night Face Up").

In *Bestiario* the exceptional experiences, narrated in disarmingly simple and straight-forward language, beset the characters with an urgency to act, an urgency that produces tension and uneasiness in the reader. The stories illuminate the mysterious and the inexplicable in man's surroundings and uncover the depths of his desires, instincts, and fears, forcing them to be recognized in a concrete, albeit hallucinatory, manner. Cortázar suggests that the real, objective, palpable world about us is but one side of a coin whose other face harbors the fantastic, the subjective, and the oneiric. It is by means of this shadow of reality, exposed to us with its fauna created and nurtured by man's imagination and subconscious alone, that Cortázar reveals the complex depths of reality, one that too often ignores the "nocturnal" side of man's life.

> I really don't know much about myself. It's you, the critics, who show me things and then I realize.
> —*Julio Cortázar*

Final del juego (End of the Game)

Final del juego, first published in 1964, is Cortázar's second collection of short stories; it contains material written between 1945 and 1962. Nine of the eighteen were previously published in 1956. The majority of the stories were written between *Bestiario*, 1951, and *Las armas secretas*, 1958 (Secret Weapons), but others postdate his first novel, *Los premios*, 1960 (*The Winners*), and even his most famous novel, *Rayuela*, 1963 (*Hopscotch*). Cortázar was not concerned with the long span of time which the variety of stories seemed to represent. As he wrote in an author's note, artistic creation is a continuous yet timeless process:

> Maurice Blanchot has shown that calendar time has little to do with the time of the main laboratory; a writer would be foolish to think that he had forever left behind a stage of his works. In any future page a new page from the past may be awaiting us, as if something had remained to be said from a stage that we thought long gone. . . .[7]

This statement serves as an accurate description of *Final del juego*, for in the eighteen short stories the reader can detect the Cortázar of *Bestiario* persisting in the theme of "otherness," as in "The Distances"; in the sensitive portrayal of the adolescent mind, as in "Bestiary"; and in the aura of mystery and tension so evident in "Circe."

In "Axolotl," "La noche boca arriba," and "Una flor amarilla" ("A Yellow Flower") the motif of "otherness," of the double, and of "figuras" endures. In "Axolotl," a man visiting an aquarium becomes so engrossed with the axolotl that he penetrates the glass and ingresses psychically into the body of that fish-like amphibian. There he remains trapped and relates his story. In many instances throughout Cortázar's literary production, water, glass, and the fish accompany the transformation of man from his present existence into another one.

"La noche boca arriba" was inspired by an accident Cortázar had in 1952 while riding a Vespa in France. In the story, a Twentieth Century man, convalescing from a motorcycle accident and a subsequent operation, has nightmares about a pre-Columbian Indian fleeing from the Aztecs. His pursuers are searching for sacrificial victims. The hallucinatory world induced by anaesthesia finally usurps the consciousness of the protagonist, for at the end of the story the two beings—modern man and pre-Columbian Indian—fuse across space and time. In a surprising twist, however, the Indian, who is initially only a dream, materializes into a corporeal being. As he is carried to the top of the sacrificial pyramid, he projects *his* dreams into the future. The torches which surround him seem to transform into red and green traffic lights. Through his desire to escape sacrifice, he attempts metamorphosis into the Twentieth Century man astride the motorcycle.

He managed to close his eyelids again, although he knew now he was not going to wake up, that he was awake, that the marvelous dream had been the other, absurd as all dreams are—a dream in which he was going through the strange avenues of an astonishing city, with green and red lights that burned without fire or smoke, on an enormous metal insect that whirred away between his legs. In the infinite lie of the dream, they had also picked him up off the ground, someone had approached him also with a knife in his hand, approached him who was lying face up, face up with his eyes closed between the bonfires on the steps.[8]

The mystery and tension of "La noche boca arriba" pervades the collection in other stories such as "Continuidad de los parques" ("Continuity of Parks"). Cortázar adds a surprise ending to this compelling and briefest of short stories. The protagonist is seated in a green velvet high-back chair in his study. He is reading a novel about an unfaithful wife, who, with her lover, calmly plots the death of her husband. As the lover leaves to carry out the homicide, the suspense of the novel, within the story, mounts for us and for the man. We both continue to read of the lover's approach to the victim's house:

He went up the three porch steps and entered. The woman's words reached him over the thudding of blood in his ears: first a blue chamber, then a hall, then a carpeted stairway. At the top, two doors. No one in the first room, no one in the second. The door of the salon, and then, the knife in hand, the light from the great windows, the high back of an armchair covered in green velvet, the head of the man in the chair reading a novel.[9]

The novel's victim, seated in the green chair, and the novel's reader, also in the green chair, become one and the same person. Reality and fiction fuse. The protagonist of a fictitious literary work is converted into one of its characters. In the novel *Rayuela*, Cortázar develops this theme into a technique and draws the reader into his fiction. He urges us to participate actively in the novel as accomplices. As we will see, this theory of the "reader-as-accomplice" serves as a key to his revolutionary structure of *Rayuela*.

Final del juego is characterized by themes which preoccupy Cortázar, for he collects rather than replaces themes. In "Los venenos" (The Poison), "Después del almuerzo" (After Lunch), and the title story, "Final del juego," he is mainly concerned with adolescence.

It is precisely, however, in stories such as "Torito"* that Cortázar establishes a new trajectory for his short stories: a more human development of characters. Cortázar does not discard his focus on the mysterious and unusual situations of most of the stories in this collection, but in "Torito" he attributes more emphasis to character portrayal.

An old boxer, bedridden in a hospital, reminisces in monologue form, about his past glories. He describes scenes from bouts with various rivals and recalls how his woman reacted to his fights. A tango was even composed to commemorate his success. Now, however, on his back, coughing and weak, at times he wishes that he could forget his past for among his memories is his final defeat in New York. At the end of the story he comments: "I wanna forget it all. Better ta sleep, even though ya dream, sometimes ya hit a good one and live it again. Like with the prince, what dough. But better

* In Spanish, "torito" means "little bull." The diminutive suffix "-ito" also connotes an endearing tone. The boxer protagonist is nicknamed "Torito."

not ta dream, kid, jus' sleep, that's the life, and no coughin', no nothin', hit the sack all night . . ."

The author, in part, conveys his sympathy by means of prose accented with colloquial Argentinean Spanish. Cortázar's literary language, especially that of his short stories, is seldom rhetorical. He uses a natural, simple sentence structure and a nontechnical vocabulary. His imagery is sensual and at times lyrical; but essentially his short story style is designed to ease the uninitiated reader into a strange world of fiction by means of subtley subversive and disarmingly conversational prose. In "Torito," however, the boxer's speech is designed even more for the ear than for the eye.

In the detectivesque story, "El movil" (The Motive) Cortázar also exposes the reader to this lower class jargon which deviates from the more universal prose in most of his short stories. The same dialect appears in other works, such as his first novel *Los premios* (1960) and his recently published *Libro de Manuel*, 1973 (Book of Manuel). In the latter, its effect is not so much that of depicting a lower class character thinking aloud, as it is of attaining rhythmic and sonorous prose by means of a playful and imaginative courtship between the author and his language.

Boxing and jazz have always fascinated Cortázar, as can be seen by the short story "Torito" as well as by the title of his second collection of miscellaneous works, *Ultimo Round* (1969). In connection with these interests Cortázar has developed his two most sympathetically conceived short-story characters in "Torito" and in "El perseguidor ("The Pursuer"). Cortázar sees both the boxer and the jazz musician as individuals who live spontaneously. Each violates an established order; the boxer physically with short aggressive jabs and retreats, the jazz musician aesthetically in improvised "takes." In his "ars poetica," Cortázar even described literary genre in boxing terms: "The novel wins by points, while the short story must win by a knockout."

In our interview, he alluded to the reason for using boxing jargon and descriptions in his works. In Latin America, he said, there is a somewhat romantic tendency to seek out esoteric and refined metaphors. He, on the other hand, has always felt that literature should contain more references to everyday realities which in themselves can be full of beauty. "A good boxing match is just as beautiful as a swan." His utilization of boxing terms corresponds not only to his enthusiasm for the sport but also to his desire to desecrate the cultivated language of Latin American literature, and thus to infuse it with life.

Most of Cortázar's stories focus on situations and plots with bizarre and often metaphysical consequences. Many deal with two facets of reality—the conscious, phenomenological world and the subconscious, psychic self. In "Torito," however, Cortázar concerns himself with a realistic portrayal of a character and his memories without oneiric or psychic overtones. There is little situational suspense in "Torito." Perhaps this is due in part to Cortázar's identification with the actual boxer described in the short story. Cortázar had carefully followed his career and confessed that "I was Justo Suárez for two hours." Later on he added, "To feel like a boxer is not at all easy."

In this same volume, Cortázar deals with another realistic facet of life in the short story "El río" (The

River)—eroticism. As the protagonist-narrator of this story falls asleep, he seems to inhabit an intermediate zone between dream and wakefulness. He talks to his silent wife, who lies at his side. His monologue weaves back and forth in time, confusing her threats of committing suicide in the Seine River, with his description of making love to her. He feels they destroy each other in their daily life together. In his somnambulant narrative, he alternates between jeering at her warnings, which makes the reader aware of her presence, and vaguely intuiting that he has heard a door slam, which suggests that she has left the room. As sleep overcomes him, he turns to make love to his wife. She tries unsuccessfully to deny him.

By means of the state of dream-wakefulness that exists in the narrator's mind, Cortázar is able to skillfully fuse two events. For in a description of dual meaning, the husband's sexual possession of his wife coincides with her drowning. In this way his desire as well as her warning seem to be fulfilled simultaneously.

> I have to dominate you slowly (you know that, I've always done it with ceremonial grace), without harming you I bend the reeds of your arms, I mold myself to the pleasure of your clenched fists, of your wide open eyes; now your rhythm finally deepens into the slow undulating movement of *moiré*, of profound bubbles rising to my face; vaguely I caress your hair spilling over the pillow, in the green shadow I see my dripping hand, and before sliding to your side, I know that they've pulled you out of the water, too late, naturally, and that you lay on the rocks by the dock surrounded by shoes and voices, naked and face up with your wet hair and your eyes wide open.[10]

This erotic dimension is emphasized more in Cortázar's novels, especially in *Rayuela* and in *Libro de Manuel* where sadistic overtones are often present. As Cortázar noted, "Evidently the sadistic component of my eroticism is very strong. It follows then that one notices it in the erotic scenes of my works."

The violent atmosphere of "El río" is characteristic of other short stories in *Final del juego*. The irrational cruelty of men which at times attains ritual intensity, is present in "Las ménades" (The Maenads), "El ídolo de las Cícladas" ("The Idol of the Cyclades"), "El movil," and "Los amigos" (The Friends). As with "Circe" and *Los reyes*, Cortázar once again alludes to Greek mythology in "El ídolo de las Cícladas" and "Las ménades."

Maenads were Greek priestesses of Bacchus, the god of feasts and the grape vine. They attended orgies to celebrate and honor the god. There, half-dressed, they painted themselves with blood, wine, and dyes and shouted frenetically. In "The Maenads" a tranquil concert is observed by a narrator who describes the slow transformation of the audience into a ritualistically violent mob. As the music awakens the instincts of the spectators, they attack the conductor, as though hypnotized into an orgiastic furor. The dispassionate narrator reminds one of the noncommittal Marcelo in "The Gates of Heaven." This type of character is developed more fully in "The Pursuer," perhaps Cortázar's best story of the third collection, *Las armas secretas*. Cortázar unfolds still another aspect of his fiction in his stories "La banda" (The Band) and "No se culpa a nadie" (No One's to Blame): the dangers of the unquestioned acceptance of one's environs. Cortázar's political consciousness is hardly ever divorced from his literary art and becomes more markedly visible in his later works,

Ultimo Round and *Libro de Manuel.* In "La banda" he creates an absurd and unbearable situation for the protagonist. It results in self-exile from his country. Critics have noted that this story could symbolize Cortázar's self-exile from Argentina after his youthful opposition to the dictatorial Perón regime. Cortázar's criticism of accepting a meaningless and superficial reality, however, is not restricted to socio-political interpretation.

In "No se culpa a nadie," he ingeniously reveals danger behind a simple experience—that of putting on a sweater. A man tries to put on a blue wool pullover but gets caught inside of it. In his efforts to free himself, he becomes even more ensnared. Blindly he stumbles around the room trying to remember if he left a window open. At one point he senses that his right hand has freed itself from the sweater and emerged into the fresh cool air; however, it seems to have acquired an independence of its own, and functions contrary to his desires to extricate himself. Finally, after persistent struggling, he falls to his knees and succeeds in emerging from the pullover. Before his eyes are five black fingernails ready to attack him: his own completely autonomous hand. He quickly retreats into the sweater as he flees from his left hand, "in order to finally arrive somewhere without a hand and a pullover, where there is only fragrant air that will envelop him and accompany him and caress him and twelve floors." Subtly, Cortázar suggests his fall from the window on the twelfth floor. After reading the story, one hastens to take an inventory of the pullovers and cardigans in the dresser drawer; unfortunately, such precautions do not ameliorate the perverse horror of a suicide caused by donning a blue pullover, nor do they erase the surrealistic image of one's own alienated hand poised to attack.

In the unique collection *Historias de cronopios y de famas*, 1962 (*Cronopios and Famas*), Cortázar once again dwells on the unexpected mysteries of daily routines. There, however, the anecdotes do not always reveal danger as in "No One's to Blame," but do incite the reader to reconsider mechanical reactions—climbing steps, crying, and winding a watch—from an unusual perspective.

Final del juego exhibits a wide range of themes and stylistic propensities in Cortázar's fiction. The game element, eroticism, the reader-as-accomplice, "otherness," and the discovery of unexpected dimensions in a recognizably mundane reality persist and evolve both in his novels and in his short stories. As in a kaleidoscope, some of the variegated fragments of *Final del juego* are recognizable from past formations; nevertheless, their fascinating combinations create new and provocative patterns.

> With "The Pursuer," there's a kind of end of a previous stage and beginning of a new world view: the discovery of fellow man.
> —*Julio Cortázar*

Las armas secretas (Secret Weapons)

Las armas secretas, published in 1968, is an anthology of five short stories. Had Cortázar produced only this book, it would have guaranteed his fame as a short-story writer. In this collection especially in "Cartas de mamá" (Letters from Mama) and "Las armas secretas," Cortázar creates a dream-like atmosphere, a trademark of his earlier stories. However, it is not those two stories which commend Cortázar to immortality as a masterful short-story writer. It is "El perseguidor" ("The Pursuer"), above all others, and perhaps "Las babas del diablo" ("Blow-Up"),[11] two stories as essentially different from one another as fraternal twins. Linked by similar themes, these two stories diverge from a common source: the creative process and its relationship to life.

> It'll never be known how this has to be told, in the first person or in the second, using the third person plural or continually inventing modes that will serve for nothing. If one might say, I will see the moon rose; or: we hurt me at the back of my eyes, and especially: you the blond woman was the clouds that race before my your his our yours their faces. What the hell.[12]

In this way Roberto Michel, the protagonist of "Las babas del diablo," begins his story. He is a French-Chilean translator living in Paris. His hobby is photography. Since this is also basically a description of Cortázar, the author's identification with his character Michel is apparent. Their occupation as translators seems to account for their concern with words. But only in part.

The *Bestiario* concept of exorcism echoes in Michel's voice: "Always tell it, get rid of that tickle in the stomach that bothers you." Seated at the window in his apartment, watching the clouds and the pigeons fly by, he unburdens himself of the adventures of a November day. During the narrative, he constantly discredits his choice of words: "Right now (what a word, *now*, what a dumb lie) . . ." He alternates between narrating in first person and in third person, as if in self-contemplation: ". . . I recited bits from Apollinaire which always get into my head whenever I pass in front of the hotel Lauzun (and at that I ought to be remembering the other poet, but Michel is an obstinate beggar) . . ."

Michel strolls through Paris to an island in the Seine and watches an older blond woman who seems to be trying to seduce an adolescent boy. Cortázar's well executed sensual descriptions capture the characters' essential traits: pure innocence in the boy, evil guile in the woman. She is thin and willowy:

> her blond hair which pared away her white bleak face—two unfair words—and put the world at her feet, horribly alone in front of her dark eyes, her eyes fell on things like two eagles, two leaps into nothingness, two puffs of green slime. I'm not describing anything, it's more a matter of trying to understand it. And I said two puffs of green slime.[13]

Michel sympathizes with the boy, reflects on his adolescent pastimes and compares the boy's nervous innocence to a "terrified bird, a Fra Filippo angel, rice pudding with milk." The scene assumes a disconcerting aura as Michel, perched on the railing, notices a man sitting in his car parked on the dock. Michel senses the woman's power over the boy, her sadistically caressing approach—"(her laugh, all at once, a whip of feathers), crushing him just by being there, smiling, one hand taking a stroll through the air." Michel imagines the final seduction of the boy in the woman's apartment. The protagonist has a strange intuition "that the woman was not looking for the boy as a lover"; nevertheless, she seemed to be dominating him in some cruel game as if she were exciting "herself for someone else, someone who in no way could be that kid." He takes a photograph of them.

When they notice him, the woman demands the film and the boy breaks away, running from the scene, "disappearing like a gossamer filament of angel-spit in the morning air." The original title of the story is taken from this passage where the boy-angel escapes, and the man with the grey hat, seated in the car—the devil—appears. Michel describes it: "filaments of angel-spittle are also called devil-spit". (The literal meaning of the spanish title is "the devil's spittle.")

The man wearing the grey hat menacingly approaches Michel. His face is powdery white like a clown's; his grimace seems to roll from one side of his mouth to the other "as though it were on wheels, independent and involuntary." His grotesque appearance startles Michel who refuses their demands for the film and walks off. It is not until several days later that he processes the film and is fascinated by the photograph of the woman and the boy. Feeling it was important that his intervention permitted the boy's flight, he tacks an enlargement of the photo on the wall.

He is strangely compelled to ignore his translation work and abandon the typewriter to stare at the photograph. Hypnotized by the scene, Michel suddenly realizes that he had innocently interfered in a much more horrible game of seduction than he had suspected. For the woman was not propositioning the boy for her own pleasure. The real boss was the homosexual with the grey hat, and the blond was his mediator: "he was not the first to send a woman in the vanguard to bring him the prisoners manacled with flowers."

The scene begins to repeat itself as the photograph, infused with life, becomes a movie before Michel's eyes. Helpless in dealing with the homosexual threat to the boy, Michel screams and moves forward *into* the photograph. As the man and woman turn toward Michel, the boy runs off. Michel has helped him escape for the second time. Confronted by the man's attack, Michel closes his eyes and cries. When he opens them, the nightmarish scene has vanished and he is seated at the window. Watching the clouds and the pigeons fly by, he relates his hallucinatory experience to us.

Michel's discontent with the appropriate choice of words and narrative perspective can now be seen as more than a literary concern with artistic expression. He has observed a scene of seduction in which he sympathized with the adolescent. The identification is complete, for Michel internalizes the horror of the episode, saves the boy, and, thus, himself. Because of his involvement as a sympathetic victim, Michel requires more than words to relate the adventure to us. He had to use a change in narrative perspective for as he observed the fleeing boy, he also watched himself. This technique suggests that, perhaps, the two characters being observed—the boy and Michel—are doubles: both escaping either physical or psychological homosexual violation. Michel, therefore, must exorcise the experience by telling the story, since it is also *his story*.

Here, as in other stories, we observe Cortázar's interest in the adolescent and the necessary exorcism of an obsession. To these, Cortázar adds three basically new themes: characters on the margin of society (homosexuals), life which is exposed as a false and superficial rendering of a hidden and unpleasant side of reality (by means of the photograph), and the creative process in its relationship to life.

Cortázar depicts characters often ostracized by society for like Michel, "Nothing pleases him more than to imagine exceptions to the rule, individuals outside the species, not-always-repugnant monsters." One may recall the Minotaur of *Los reyes*, a beast-man, inhabiting the outskirts of society and his species, a non-conformist, hidden away, and yet portrayed sympathetically by Cortázar. Homosexuals fit into this category—as do jazz musicians, insane people and "cronopios"*—all of whom Cortázar portrays in his literature.

In "Los buenos servicios" ("At Your Service"), another story in this same collection, Cortázar mingles two themes—marginal man and false reality—to create an interesting tale. Madame Francinet, the protagonist, is an old servant woman, masterfully portrayed as innocent and forthright in her relationships. Cortázar commented that he had come to know many old women like her in Paris for they came to clean the house and often conversed with him. The short story's Madame Francinet is employed to babysit for dogs in the home of a wealthy family during one of their parties. There she meets some of the guests in the kitchen and converses with one of them, Monsieur Bébé, the only one who treats her kindly.

On another occasion, she is asked to assume the

* Cronopios is the word that Cortázar coins to describe beings which resemble human beings of a certain type—intuitive, creative, impractical, spontaneous.

role of mother at the funeral of a young man; he is a friend of the same wealthy family. She arrives at the wake and discovers that the deceased is Bébé. Her feigned anguish is transformed into authentic sorrow as she remembers her first encounter with him. The behavior and sympathy of this ingenuous old woman, however, is ironic. Not only is she the only person who genuinely mourns Bébé's death, but also she is the sole character heedless of the fact that the men whom she met at the party, and again at the wake, are a group of homosexuals.

Reality is not at all what it seems to Madame Francinet. More importantly, however, it is also not what the reader surmised; for it is only by accumulated insinuations during the story that one intuits the false reality at the end. Bébé is blond, pale, wears a white suit in the middle of winter and has fragile white hands; his companions all share childish female names, Nina and Loulou; Nina, although a man, is referred to once as "she"; the men playfully scuffle in the kitchen; Bébé can confide in Madame Francinet because, as he says, she is not young and not a risk; the men are excitable and emotional, laughter turns into hysterical tears; and, finally, near the end of the story, one of the men refers to another as a "whore." Since during the story, however, these hints are very subtle, Madame Francinet in her innocence does not perceive them. The reader must be sensitive to the author's covert intent in order to capture the false reality that surrounds Madame Francinet, and by association, perhaps us.

When asked to explain his attitude toward homosexuality as a topic in several of his short stories and novels, Cortázar answered at length with a history of homosexuality as it progressed from ancient times through persecutions to the present stage of social ostracism. Although he decried corruption of a minor, in either homosexual or heterosexual seduction, he welcomed a more tolerant attitude toward homosexuality. He noted uncomfortably that this attitude is more rapidly becoming a reality in capitalist than in socialist societies:

> The attitude toward homosexuality has to be a very broad and open one because the day in which homosexuals don't feel like corralled beasts, or like persecuted animals or like beings that everyone makes fun of, they'll assume a much more normal way of life and fulfill themselves erotically and sexually without harming anyone and by being happy as much as is possible as homosexual males or females.

The creative process and its relationship to life is the principal theme of "El perseguidor," the longest and perhaps the most successful of Cortázar's short stories. He has many times commented on the importance of this narrative, and he feels that it is a turning point in his literary career. For the first time he wrote of an existential problem which would appear again in his novels *Los premios* and *Rayuela.* In this short story Cortázar begins to observe and fathom the dilemmas of fellow man.

Cortázar notes that "El perseguidor" had been written almost by a miracle of fate. He had been searching for a protagonist for a short story that would not be fantastic, when he read in a Paris newspaper the obituary of Charlie Parker, the black jazz musician to whom the story is dedicated. After writing the first episode of the story in Paris, he had a mental block and could not continue; so he stuffed the papers into a drawer. Months later while in Geneva on business for UNESCO, he found the papers, in his briefcase, reread them, and began to work on the story again. In two days he had finished writing one of his most successful works. "I realized several years later that if I hadn't written 'El perseguidor,' I would have been incapable of writing *Rayuela.* 'El perseguidor' is a miniature *Rayuela.*"

Charlie Parker's life inspired Cortázar to reincarnate him as the protagonist, Johnny Carter. In fact, many of the events in the story actually parallel Charlie Parker's career as a jazz saxophonist and his life as a drug addict. Cortázar, however, focuses on two characters, the musician Johnny Carter and the jazz critic Bruno. Each is concerned with artistic creativity and its relevance to life; however, Johnny is an involved and anguished creator, whereas Bruno is an analytical spectator.

For Johnny Carter, music is a mode of expression that far surpasses his inadequate grasp of words. Through music, Johnny enriches his life. Rather than using music as an escape from the time that surrounds him, he believes that music puts him *into* that time. Playing the saxophone, he explains, compresses vast experience into a few moments. He compares it to a Métro ride where, in a span of one minute and a half between subway stops, he manages to experience at least fifteen minutes of thoughts. "Bruno, if I could only live all the time like in those moments, or like when I'm playing and the time changes then, too."

Johnny disdains conventional time, watches and daily schedules, as well as traditional life styles. With his "metaphysical" music, as Bruno defines it, Johnny seems to explore himself, "to bite into the reality that escapes every day." He cannot understand how others can feel so "sure of themselves" in this conventional existence, like the self-satisfied doctors at Camarillo, the mental institution where he convalesced. He sees holes in daily existence through which he intuits that there must be something more authentic than the glimpses of exciting facets of life exposed to him by his music. These tantalizing glimpses are destroyed by the alcohol and drugs of his sordid, everyday life.

After reading Bruno's biography of him, Johnny comments on the critic's failure to understand him. He notes the critic's ingenious word plays—sax and sex—and the erroneous comparison of his music to a communion with God: "On top of everything, I don't buy your God . . . I don't wanna know nothing about that goddamned uniformed doorman, that opener of doors in exchange for a goddamned tip, that . . ."

Bruno perceives the two sides of Johnny's being: his creative genious and his sordid battle with life. He is confounded, although not anguished, by Johnny's plight. As a mere critic of music, and not a creator, he envies Johnny's talent but not his existential anguish. He pities "poor Johnny trying to move forward with his decapitated sentences," searching for a life that cannot exist unless everyone turns crazy, feeding his misery on drugs and alcohol. Bruno could never deny the security of his everyday "coffee and cigarettes" to pursue a futile and dangerous desire like Johnny's. And yet Bruno admits:

> Johnny was no victim, not persecuted as everyone thought, as I'd even insisted upon in my biography of him. . . . I

> know now that's not the way it is, that Johnny pursues and is not pursued, that all the things happening in his life are the hunter's disaster, not the accidents of the harassed animal.[14]

In Bruno's confused eulogy, respect and pity intermingle. To him Johnny is both the pursuer of a dimension to life that we and Bruno seem to ignore and the helpless "hunter with no arms and legs."

In Johnny and in Bruno, Cortázar has set forth the creator's dilemmas: a search for a bridge to a richer, more meaningful existence and its effective communication to fellow man. Cortázar himself identifies both with the writer—as creator and critic—and with the jazz musician. He himself plays amateur jazz trumpet and is an aficionado of jazz. In this story as well as in the novels *Rayuela* and *Libro de Manuel*, Cortázar pursues both the search for authenticity and its communication. The dilemma does not concern one jazz musician and one critic, however, but the very nature of the relationship between artistic expression and life.

It is, therefore, in *Las armas secretas* that Cortázar begins to question the two sides of the same coin: the connection between life and its mysteries in "Cartas de mamá" and "Las armas secretas"; the relationship between false and visible reality and its actual hidden meanings in "Las babas del diablo" and "Los buenos servicios"; and the relevance of creativity and its expression to the enrichment of existence in "El perseguidor." Although technical virtuosity is a characteristic of this volume, it is surely the human qualities of Johnny's search for a more bearable existence, his anguished failures, and his groping to express his pursuit that pay homage to Cortázar as a "pursuer" of bridges between literature and life.

> The *Cronopios* is my most playful book, really a game, a fascinating game, very amusing; it was almost like a tennis match. There was no serious intention.
> —*Julio Cortázar*

Historias de cronopios y de famas (Cronopios and Famas: An Interlude)

Between 1952 and 1959, Julio Cortázar wrote anecdotes which he later entitled *Historias de cronopios y de famas*, 1962. The four different sections were written at varying times and in diverse places—Italy, France, Argentina—and not as a unified book. A friend in Argentina read the anecdotes about cronopios, a section which Cortázar had run off on his own mimeograph machine as private editions for friends. He wanted to publish it; however, since the selection was rather short, he asked Cortázar for more brief texts. In that way the other three sections were added to complete this final volume, a joyful interlude in Cortázar's short story production.

In Argentina the book was received with mixed emotions: the poets respected it; the critics were shocked at such a lack of seriousness. It seemed as if Cortázar, after many stories and his first novel, *Los premios*, had abandoned his previous themes and style for a frivolous fantasy. Closely observed, however, nothing could be more erroneous than that assumption. *Historias de cronopios y de famas*, in fact, is an important transition between his earlier fiction and the works which followed, especially *Rayuela.* There is a new ingredient here, an imaginatively playful humor in the face of an absurd existence.

Before *Historias de cronopios y de famas*, Cortázar had already questioned reality as false and superficial, and praised creativity as a means to an enriched experience in life. He had revealed another facet of man by emphasizing his subconscious desires, phobias, and hallucinations. In *Historias de cronopios y de famas,* Cortázar unknowingly gives us a lesson in how to make humdrum existence bearable and even exciting; how to use our imagination creatively to mold life to our desires; how to provoke everyday reality into yielding unexpected marvels.

The opening selection, entitled "Manual de Instrucciones" ("The Instruction Manual"), clearly sets forth Cortázar's intent. He designates existence as a hard brick of habit that needs to be softened.

> The job of having to soften up the brick every day, the job of cleaving a passage through the glutinous mass that declares itself to be the world, to collide every morning with the same narrow rectangular space with the disgusting name, filled with doggy satisfaction that everything is probably in its place, the same woman beside you, the same shoes, the same taste of the same toothpaste, the same sad houses across the street. . . .[15]

He challenges us to break out of the "glass brick" like a bull. Cortázar maintains that we remain unaware of our everyday gestures, like turning the doorknob or saying goodbye: daily reflexes which could "transform everything." Habit has reduced everything to a "suitable smoothness," keeping us from feeling the metal pulse of a teaspoon that we use to stir the coffee. We fail to "feel" life, we only experience its "sameness."

He seems to exhort us to be more sensitive to our daily surroundings, "Don't believe that the telephone is going to give you the numbers you try to call, why should it?" A walk to the corner to buy the newspaper can be an adventure, if we so desire:

> When the door opens and I lean over the stairwell, I'll know that the street begins down there; not the already accepted matrix, not the familiar houses, not the hotel across the street: the street, that busy wilderness which can tumble upon me like a magnolia any minute, where the faces will come to life when I look at them, when I go just a little bit further, when I smash minutely against the pie dough of the glass brick and stake my life while I press forward step by step to go pick up the newspaper at the corner.[16]

In order to discover the marvelous treasures of mundane life, one must abandon certain traits which civilization has imposed on us: reason and pragmatism. In their place Cortázar would have us sharpen our imagination, use our inclination to play, dispose ourselves to adventure, and value absurdity. He suggests that we lack an uninhibited child-like perspective of reality. Life, viewed by a child, is made to seem magical, new, and exotic. Precisely because of its attack of adult logic, *Historias de cronopios y de famas* is Cortázar's most consistently surrealistic book.

Cortázar has always felt the influence of the French surrealists who strove for the same results in life, art, and literature as those set forth in *Historias de cronopios y de famas.* At the University of Cuyo in Argentina between 1945 and 1946 Cortázar taught French literature, including surrealism. In 1949, he called surrealism "a living corpse," a world view of reality which, far from dead, lived on, although disguised, in daily life. As late as 1963, in an interview, Cortázar refused to be classified as a surrealist, although at the same time he conceded an honored place to several of its proponents: "In my library you will find books by Crevel, Jacques Vaché, Arthur Cravan (but don't catalogue me as a surrealist because of that!)"[17] More recently, however, he has observed surrealism to be an inextinguishable force in certain men, "perhaps in all men." In *Historias de cronopios y de famas*, Cortázar seems to urge us to throw off the handcuffs of logic and to live surrealistically by means of desire, imagination and child-like adventures into fantasy.

In an interview, Cortázar explained the genesis of "The Instruction Manual" section:

> Another part of the book, "The Instruction Manual," I wrote after I got married, when Aurora and I went to live in Italy for a while. You have Aurora to blame for these texts. One day, mounting an endless staircase in a museum, out of breath, she said suddenly: "The trouble is that this is a staircase for going down." I loved that phrase. So I said to Aurora: "One ought to write some instructions about how to go up and down a staircase."[18]

Cortázar's instructions force us to think about our emotions—crying and being afraid; our cultural values —understanding famous paintings; our habitual actions —combing hair and climbing stairs; and some unusual pastimes—dissecting a ground owl, or killing ants in

Rome. His imaginative explanations are humorous, and at times, shocking. His "Examples of How to Be Afraid" includes the following:

The doctor finished his examination and his conclusions are very reassuring to us. His cordial and somber voice precedes the medicines, prescriptions for which he is writing out at the moment, seated behind his desk. Every once in a while he raises his head and smiles, to cheer us up. We don't have a thing to worry about, we'll be better inside of a week. We sit at ease in our easy chair, happy, and look idly and distractedly about the room. In the shadowed area beneath the desk, suddenly we see the doctor's legs. The trousers are pulled up to just above the knees and he's wearing women's stockings.[19]

Above all "The Instruction Manual" provokes one to view habitual practices in a new perspective. In the "Preambulo a las instrucciones para dar cuerda al reloj" ("Preamble to the Instructions on How To Wind a Watch"), Cortázar transforms a practical invention that we use every day into a machine that uses us. He describes a wristwatch as a "tiny flowering hell, a wreath of roses, a dungeon of air." It is a "minute stonecutter" which binds us to implacable time. When given a gift of a watch, one is unaware of its demands: to wind it; to obsessively check the exact time in every jewelry window, on every radio program, or with the telephone service; to fear that it will be stolen, or break if it falls; to wonder if the brand is the best; to compare it with others. "They aren't giving you a watch, you are the gift, they're giving you yourself for the watch's birthday."

The entries in the second section of the anthology "Ocupaciones raras" ("Unusual Occupations") are similar to short stories. The intensity with which the characters—the family that lives on Humboldt Street—undertake their strange occupations produces an atmosphere of expectations.

Their adventures are usually absurd, illogical, often dangerous, and yet humorous. They could be described as "happenings": illogical events that reflect an absurd world in order to emphasize man's precarious condition. "Happenings" are characterized by visual provocation, spontaneity and an opening onto the marvelous in life. Although the "happening: is an art form, it cannot be placed in a museum, like a painting or a sculpture. It is an event limited by the time in which it occurs and unique in its need to provoke."[20]

In one of the anecdotes, the family invades a wake and takes over. They weep with exaggerated grief. The family thus caricatures the "craftier forms of hypocrisy" exhibited by friends and relatives of the deceased who often feign sorrow.

In the selection "Correos y telecomunicaciones" ("Postal and Telegraph Service"), with the help of a relative, the family receives appointments in the post office. They begin "handling things, adapting procedures to their principles and predilections." One sister gives away colored balloons at the stamp window; the father serves shots of vodka and veal cutlets at another window. When the police invade the premises, the mother is flying paper airplanes made from telegrams and money order forms. A member of the family explains: "We sang the national anthem and retired in good order; I saw a little girl, third in line at the stamp window, crying, when she realized it was already too late for them to give her a balloon."

Amidst the game-like atmosphere of "Conducta en los velorios" ("Our Demeanor at Wakes"), "Correos y telecomunicaciones," "Pérdida y recuperación del pelo" ("The Loss and Recovery of the Hair"), other anecdotes such as "Los posatigres" ("The Tiger Lodgers") and "Simulacra" describe dangerous endeavors. The gothic terror of castles and dungeons, mystery and menace, characterizes "Simulacra."

In the garden in front of the house, the family gleefully erects a platform with a gibbet, rack, and wheel. The construction begins quite naturally on a "Sunday afternoon after the raviolis." At first the neighbors think that the family is enlarging the house with a new floor or two. As the construction progresses, however, and the sisters gather in the garden to practice a few wolf howls, bystanders realize that gallows are being built. They protest the undertaking and threaten the family.

When the police arrive, one of the sisters convinces the officer that the family is on its own property and engaged in a "project only the use of which could vest it with illegal character . . ." At nightfall the family dines by the light of a lamp on the platform, surrounded by a crowd of spiteful neighbors. The wheel of the rack creaks and the gallows rope swings above them in the breeze. As the happy family disperses after coffee, the spectators begin to go off "as if they were disappointed or something." Ironically, the mob that felt threatened by the gallows was also attracted to its dangers. Like Romans at the arena, they were frustrated when there was no violence. The family, nevertheless, had enjoyed itself immensely during this completely useless, although provocative, "happening."

In the next section entitled "Material plástico" ("Unstable Stuff"), Cortázar's anecdotes touch briefly on familiar subjects and objects—secretaries, bicycles, mirror, geography, easy chairs—but always with a bizarre twist. There, again, Cortázar manifests his surrealism by concentrating on unusual perspectives, imagination, and exceptions. Perhaps the title of one of the anecdotes best describes one of Cortázar's main themes in this book: "A Small Story Tending To Illustrate The Uncertainty Of The Stability Within Which We Like To Believe We Exist, Our Laws Could Give Ground To The Exceptions, Unforeseen Disaster, Or Improbabilities; And I Want To See You There."

This assertion closely resembles that of Alfred Jarry, a French precursor of surrealism. In his book about a Doctor Faustroll, who is half hero and half troll, he described the science of exceptions or "pataphysics":

> Pataphysics will examine the laws governing exceptions, and will explain the universe supplementary to this one, or, less ambitiously, will describe a universe which can be—and perhaps should be—envisaged in the place of the traditional one, since the laws that have been discovered in the traditional universe are also correlations of exceptions, albeit more frequent ones, but in any case accidental exceptions, that possess no longer even the virtue of originality.[21]

Cortázar admires Jarry's personal and literary attitude. He feels as Jarry does that serious matter can be explored by means of humor. Cortázar mentions "pataphysics" in several of his works—*Rayuela* and *La vuelta al día en ochenta mundos*—bases many short stories on the unusual exceptions to every day existence, and devotes a section of *Historias de cronopios y de famas* to "Material Plástico."

The title epitomizes Cortázar's interest in the bizarre—the odd, the fanciful, the grotesque. In one of these episodes, in the Jacinto family's house, we find an easy chair to die in. The children often invite unsuspecting visitors to sit in it. Another anecdote tells of a man who is capable of abstracting details from reality. He can concentrate on ears, buttons, and with an x-ray type vision, on oranges that are being digested. In still another tale, a decapitated man is not buried because of a gravediggers' strike. He wanders about headless, slowly recovering his senses of smell, taste, sight and hearing, despite his condition.

In "Qué tal, López" ("How's It Going, López?") Cortázar criticizes the habits we wear like a worn out glove. A gentleman meets a friend and greets him. He thinks that he is saying hello, "but the greeting already exists and this good gentleman is only putting the greeting on for the umpteen-hundredth time." Cortázar maintains that fear of the unknown causes us to adhere to worn out gestures in life. "The genuinely new creates either fear or wonderment." He seems to exhort us to take notice of disconcerting situations for they help to define us. "When the shoe pinches, it's a good sign."

In the last section of this unusual anthology, Cortázar creates a special being—the cronopio—who lives spontaneously and playfully like a child. The cronopio seems to be a product of Cortázar's desire to have man free himself of reason and pragmatism: perhaps he is Cortázar's answer to an absurdly ordered and unimaginative existence.

The word "cronopio" was coined as a result of a

concert that Cortázar attended in the Théatre des Champs Élysées. There he envisioned creatures that he called cronopios, a kind of amorphous microbe floating in the air. He endowed them with human characteristics and began to write anecdotes about their adventures.

Cortázar published his first article using the new word "cronopio" ten years before the appearance of the book *Historias de cronopios y de famas*. "Louis enormísimo cronopio" (Louis, the Supreme Cronopio) was included in the magazine *Buenos Aires literaria* in 1952, as a commentary on a jazz concert by Louis Armstrong held in Paris on November 9th of that year. In the very first paragraph of the article, Cortázar reserves a special place for cronopios and their creative artistry:

> It seems as if the bossy little bird, better known as God, breathed life into the first man to animate him and give him spirit. If Louis had been there instead of the birdy, man would have turned out much better . . . A world that might have begun with Picasso instead of ending with him, would be a world exclusively for cronopios; and on every corner cronopios would dance tregua and catala, and perched on the lamppost, there would be Louis blowing for hours, causing huge pieces of stars made from syrup and raspberries to fall from the sky, so the kids and the dogs could eat it all up.[22]

This article, collected in 1967 in *La vuelta al día en ochenta mundos*, contains some of Cortázar's most interesting imagery as well as a new world of unusual and yet strangely familiar creatures. For at the same concert are the cronopio-jazz fans, the esperanza-ushers, and the famas, who came by mistake or because the tickets were costly.

In the section entitled "Cronopios y famas," the tales are an enticing mixture of the mundane and the magical. The social order of the cronopios, esperanzas, and famas, is described in an accumulation of details about their customs. Cortázar lures us into a world that we recognize as our own. These creatures dance, go shopping, wear watches, eat and drink, travel, are businessmen, workers and explorers, drive automobiles, and receive medical degrees. They engage in recognizably logical activities, visit familiar places and use the same mundane objects and products that we do, like toothpaste.

And yet, the following words are neologisms, all of which are found in the very first selection entitled "Costumbres de los famas" ("Normal Behavior of the Famas"): fama, tregua, catala, cronopios, esperanzas, espera, and pez de flauta. Although several of them actually exist as words in the Spanish language, their meanings apply very indirectly to the literary context in which they are found: tregua (truce or respite), espera (wait), and catala (which has no meaning) are dances in Cortázar's book; fama (fame), esperanza (hope) and cronopio (which has no Spanish equivalent) are the inhabitants of this fictitious world, and pez de flauta literally means "a flute-fish." In our interview, Cortázar recalled that cronopio, fama, and esperanza came to him with the visualization of these creatures; whereas, catala and tregua were words with a certain "swing" to them, somewhat as in Lewis Carroll's "Jabberwocky."

There are, therefore, familiar customs, products, and places intermingled with strange new words. The normal events and objects allow the reader to capture the sense of the passage; whereas the neologisms create an exotic atmosphere and a curiosity in the reader. He wants to discover what these words actually mean.

The three main characters in "Cronopios y famas" seem to correspond to societal types, who have been given the generic names of fama, esperanza and cronopio. Cortázar asserts that a societal cross-section was entirely unintentional. At times, however, these characters are described as if they were microbes.

The famas seem to represent the leaders and the employers, whose lives are regulated by logic and pragmatism. Famas, who are proper, authoritarian and businesslike, only speak after much deliberation. They also prepare far in advance for a trip. Generous by nature, the fama helps the esperanzas when they get in trouble. Since he doesn't realize, however, that the esperanzas need continual help, the fama goes off to his club and feels satisfied with his charity. The dances of the famas are tregua and catala. Although Cortázar would certainly not agree, perhaps the name "fama" relates to their success in a world ruled by reason.

The esperanzas seem to designate the followers and the employees, who are submerged in trivial details and record keeping. They are the ushers and the librarians, those who "hope"—and thus, perhaps, their name—to become something else. "Esperanzas are sedentary. They let things and people slide by them. They're like statues one has to go visit. They never take the trouble." Those "sparkling microbes," as Cortázar describes them, dance espera or "the wait."

The most imaginative of all are the cronopios, "those wet green objects . . . those green prickly humid things." They are disorganized and enthusiastically partake of imaginative and unusual adventures. Cronopios never plan ahead for trips. Not generous by nature, and rather self-centered, they ignore esperanzas in need of help. "These cronopios do not even look at the esperanza, being completely occupied with staring at the devil's spittle." Like Roberto Michel who is the protagonist of "Las babas del diablo," Louis Armstrong, and Johnny Carter of "El perseguidor," the artists, the creators and those who value imaginative and spontaneous endeavors are defined as cronopios.

Many cronopios are easily possessed by gaiety. In "Lo particular y lo universal" ("The Particular and the Universal"), a cronopio stands on his balcony brushing his teeth. Enthralled by the morning sun and the passing clouds, he happily squeezes the pink toothpaste all over his toothbrush and also over the side of the balcony. The famas standing below are not at all pleased with his scandalous behavior. They upbraid him for being messy and wasteful.

In anecdotes like "Relojes" ("Clocks"), the cronopio is the epitome of impracticality. A cronopio notices that a fama carefully winds his wall clock daily. The cronopio goes home and invents a wild artichoke clock which he hangs on the wall. Its leaves indicate the hours. When he wants to know the time, the cronopio simply plucks a leaf from left to right. "When he reaches the center, time cannot be measured, and in the infinite violet-rose of the artichoke heart the cronopio finds great contentment. Then he eats it with oil, vinegar, and salt and puts another clock in the hole."

The cronopio has invented a "surrealist object": an object liberated from its practical and traditional functions which are sacrificed to the imagination and desire of the inventor. The cronopio is as creative as surrealists like Meret Oppenheim, who covered a cup, saucer and spoon with fur; Man Ray who afixed tacks to the bottom of a flat-iron; and Francis Picabia and Marcel Duchamp who designed marvelously intricate, albeit non-functional, machines. All of these inventions and objects, including the wild artichoke clock, assert the cronopios imaginative power over phenomenological reality. His disregard for reason and pragmatism prevails.

This anthology ends with the world of the cronopios. They are nonconformists who, in a cheerful denial of pragmatism unleash fantasy. At times their adventures seem to be children's fairy tales—magical and free. In fact, cronopios restore the childlike perspective to reality that we as civilized adults suppress. They are child-men at play. And yet, it is precisely by means of their seemingly frivolous adventures that Cortázar exposes that carefree part of us that we ignore. For most of us are famas and esperanzas, not cronopios. The critics' first impression of *Historias de cronopios y de famas* as a frivolous work captured only a part of the book's essence. For although Julio Cortázar may deny any intentional seriousness, the playful and fanciful facade of *Historias de cronopios y de famas* barely hides a serious message for rational, perhaps too rational, humanity. "The cronopios is a great game for me; it's my pleasure," declared Cortázar. Unfortunately, he then added that it is the kind of book that one should write but once.

At heart I'm not pessimistic, I'm realistic.
—*Julio Cortázar*

Todos los fuegos el fuego (All Fires the Fire)

In 1966, Cortázar's last collection of eight short stories was published. *Todos los fuegos el fuego* appeared, therefore, after Cortázar's first two novels, *Los premios* (1960) and *Rayuela* (1963), and before his last two novels, *62: Modelo para armar*, 1968, (*62: A Model Kit*) and *Libro de Manuel* (1973). In this anthology, Cortázar's view of life is once again present: reality and fantasy in close association and interaction. Realism is emphasized in "Reunión" ("Meeting") and "La señorita Cora" ("Nurse Cora"), fantasy in "Instrucciones para John Howell" ("Instructions for John Howell") and an intermingling of both in the title story.

In the unusual story "La autopista del sur" ("The Southern Thruway"), Cortázar focuses on a commonplace occurrence—a traffic jam on a major highway south of Paris. On a Sunday afternoon in August, crowds are returning to the city from the countryside. The drivers and passengers begin to talk to each other through open windows from car to car. During brief, and then gradually longer, periods of immobility, the people become acquainted with one another. When the cars move forward, slightly and infrequently, the same people seem to maintain a solid block, advancing or stopping as a group. Once in a while a "stranger" approaches from an unknown place in the traffic jam with news about the tie-up.

At nightfall the people settle into routine necessities and pastimes: they share food, sleep, and disappear discreetly in to the night to relieve themselves.

Almost everyone listened to the radio and the boys in the Simca had theirs at full blast singing along with a twist, rocking the car with their gyrations; the nuns were saying their rosaries; the little boy in the Taunus had fallen asleep with his face against the window, the toy car in his hand.[23]

The passengers, thrown together by a chance traffic jam, become inhabitants of a section of the highway. They send members of their group out to unknown areas on the highway and to the surrounding countryside in search of water, food, and information. By means of these forays, the people learn that other groups have formed along the highway. They become suspicious of strangers who pass by to trade goods.

In the newly formed cellular group, problems arise. Food is scarce and a fight breaks out over the theft of some precious water. The young care for the aged, the children play and argue with each other, and leaders emerge in the group. The days pass, it rains a little, and the cars advance slightly; but once again they come to a halt.

Although the radio announces an emergency situation on the highway, only one solitary helicopter flies by and no other help is in sight. The group tries to adapt to the strange situation. The Peugot is transformed into an ambulance for the sick people. A driver commits suicide by drinking poison and is found slouched over the steering wheel. Attempts to establish contact with people alongside the highway are met with hostility. There is even a burgeoning black market for water.

The seasons in the story rapidly change. The sweltering sun of an August day gives way to cold weather. The people wrap themselves in blankets and turn on the heaters. They fear that the batteries will run down. One day, at noon, snow begins to fall.

Amidst the vicissitudes of survival, there are small pleasures:

> At night, the groups entered another life, secret and private; doors would open or close to let a frozen figure in or out; not one looked at the others; eyes were blind as darkness itself. Some kind of happiness endured here and there under dirty blankets, in hands with overgrown fingernails, in bodies smelling of unchanged clothes and of days cramped inside.[24]

As the weather dissipates, the life cycle continues. The young woman in the Dauphine tells the engineer from the Peugot 404 that she is pregnant with his child. The old woman in the ID Citroen dies.

Suddenly, the columns of cars begin to advance. The engineer and the woman in the Dauphine, each in their own car, glance at one another with hopes of reaching Paris—to be able to bathe and eat, drink, and sleep on clean sheets. The rows of cars do not advance as a block and so friends are replaced by strangers. The group disperses as the engineer, thinking and hoping that he sees a familiar face, recalls the routines of their existence during the traffic jam. Finding it difficult to break out of a way of life imposed upon him by the lengthy tie-up, he nostalgically remembers the nights with the woman in the Dauphine, the stars and the clouds, life itself.

> And on the car's antenna the red-cross flag waved madly, and you moved at 55 miles an hour toward the lights that kept growing, not knowing why all this hurry, why this

mad race in the night among unknown cars, where no one knew anything about the others, where everyone looked straight ahead, only ahead.[25]

In "La autopista del sur" a chance situation, an exception, by means of an exaggeration becomes the rule. Complete strangers form a societal group and settle into daily functions and habits with alarming ease. The people become as entrapped in the chrysallis of the new yet familiar order as they must have been in their daily lives. The traffic jam assumes bizarre proportions for it lasts days, months and even seasons. When it ends, only the memories of ephemeral friendships prevail. One's life seems but a series of adjustments to habitual existence. Man will always reduce himself, even in exceptional circumstances, to the routine life.

In discussing this story, Cortázar realized that the ending was somewhat like that of his first novel *Los premios.* In that story, as well, after a long trip, in that case aboard a ship, the people disperse at the end. That's how it really is, he commented; one makes friends and then after the trip is over, after an exchange of family photographs and one postcard, you never see each other again.

There are two techniques that Cortázar employs in "La autopista del sur" which reinforce the theme of the story. The characters have no names; they are designated throughout by their material possessions—the car—as the man in the Caravell or the engineer in the Peugot 404. In this way they are "everyman," nameless you and me. They can, thus, serve Cortázar's intent of being strangers to each other at the start and circularly assuming the same anonymity at the story's close. They become even further dehumanized at the end of the tale where they definitively become "the Dauphine" or "the Taunus."

Another stylistic device in the story involves the use of very long sentences which approximate the rhythm of the cars incessant stopping and starting. This occurs at the beginning with a sentence that occupies an entire page.

In another story, "La señorita Cora," Cortázar also exhibits stylistic virtuosity. The first person narrative perspective is successively transferred from one character to another. In this way the reader is constantly being exposed to the minds of various characters as they think and speak about their situation. This peripatetic "I" narrative is unique in that Cortázar never directly designates the speakers by name or by the use of quotation marks in dialogue. Nevertheless, the reader is able to capture the shifts in narrative point of view. Cortázar notes that he had wanted to see "if one could write so as to change the narrative point of view within the sentences." The following passage clearly flows from nurse Cora to the ailing adolescent, who thinks his mother is at his side, to nurse Cora again:

> . . . You think I'm your Mama. You're real handsome, you know, with that turned up nose and those lashes like curtains, you look older now that you're pale. Now you won't get red for nothing, right, my poor little thing. It hurts, Mama, it hurts, here, let me take off that weight they put on me, I have something on my stomach that weighs so much and hurts, Mama, tell the nurse to take it off. Yes, dear, it'll go away soon, keep still a little, how can you be so strong, I'm going to have to call María Luisa to help me.[26]

As can be seen in the previous passage, "Nurse Cora" is a story about an adolescent boy hospitalized for an operation. Although his mother still views him as a child, Pablo finds it very difficult to control his attraction to the nurse Cora. A flirtation ensues with embarrassment for Pablo and contradictory feelings for Cora. She tries to remain uninvolved, to care for Pablo only as a patient, and yet she feels her facade dissolve before him. He, in turn, is both attracted to her and annoyed at her for treating him like a child. When Cora finally removes her mask of indifference, it is too late. Pablo rejects her and calls for his mother. He dies as Miss Cora pleads with him to call her just plain Cora.

The themes and attitudes expressed in "La señorita Cora" appear in Cortázar's novel *62: Modelo para armar*. There, one finds an allusion to a relationship between a female anesthetist and an adolescent, a confused maternal-lover attitude on the part of the woman and her resultant guilt over the death of the boy. Cortázar insists, however that this was only an analogous situation and that the characters of Hélène and the boy in *62: Modelo para armar* and the nurse and Pablo in "La señorita Cora" were quite different. Yet he admits a fascination since youth with the relationship between a female doctor and a male patient, a curious mixture of pain and care. He recalls what he terms the "sadism" of a young female dentist whom he visited when he was an adolescent. He, like Pablito in the story, was strangely attracted to her. Referring to "Nurse Cora," Cortázar explains, "It is one of the short stories that I'm happy I wrote. It made me suffer a lot because I identified closely with the character of the young boy."

In "Reunión" Cortázar captures the personal experience of a guerrilla during the Cuban Revolution. Although many of Cortázar's stories may have political interpretations, they usually are not overtly political in their plots or themes. "Reunión" is a departure from that norm. Here, as well as in his last novel, *Libro de Manuel*, Cortázar openly confronts and describes the realities of politics and revolution in the world.

The story is based on a passage from a book by Ernesto Che Guevara, *Episodes of the Revolutionary War* which portrays the landing of the guerrillas in Cuba. In "Meeting" Cortázar's protagonist is Che Guevara, although his name is never mentioned. He relates the experiences of his group as they land on the island and make their way toward the mountains to unite with Fidel Castro, called Luis in the story.

Cortázar blends realism and lyricism in "Reunión." The protagonist communicates his sentiments about death, hunger, and the fear that Luis has been killed before he is able to reach the safety of the hills. Amid furtively smoked cigarettes and spongy biscuits, the narrator recalls passages from Mozart's *The Hunt* and memories of life in his native Argentina. In this way, Cortázar pays homage to a fellow Argentinean, Che, who died for the Cuban Revolution and, at the same time, the author links his own hopes for a new social order to his own country, Argentina.

At the end of "Reunión," the protagonist reaches the hills where he is reunited with Luis. Seated under a tree with his friend, the narrator sees a star through the branches, a small blue star in the center of the design, surely symbolic of hope.

Two other stories in the collection are concerned

with "designs"—in this case "figures" as Cortázar calls them—"Todos los fuegos el fuego" and "El otro cielo" ("The Other Heaven"). In both, people, events, and places relate to each other across time and space forming "figures" or constellations, mirror images or parallel circumstances which have no logical explanation.

Cortázar's "figures" originally appeared as early as in his first collection of short stories, *Bestiario*, where in "Lejana," Alina Reyes is strangely attracted to her double, the beggar woman in Budapest. In his first novel, *Los premios*, Cortázar delivers poetic monologues in which he describes Persio's effort to understand individual events as part of a great constellation or "figure." He suggests that we, like stars, form part of a fixed design.

> He [Persio] is sure that an order scarcely perceivable by analogy governs the chaos which includes a singer taking leave of his brother and a wheelchair embellished by a chrome crank; like the dark certainty that there exists a central point in which every discordant element can finally become visible as a spoke in a wheel.[27]

Cortázar is constantly relating characters—the Maga and Talita in *Rayuela*; places—Rome and Paris in "Todos los fuegos el fuego"; periods of time—Paris in 1870 to Buenos Aires in 1940 in "El otro cielo"; and events—an escape by female prisoners in La Plata to guerrilla activities in Paris in *Libro de Manuel*. This consistant technique is an essential component of his view of reality, for he feels that our personal actions may be regulated by forces unknown to us that cause us to interact in patterned structures that negate our individual freedom.

"Figures" appear over and over again in his short

stories like "The Night Face Up," in his articles like "Marcelo del Campo, o más encuentros a deshora" ("Marcel Duchamp, or More Fortuitous Encounters") in *Ultimo Round*, and definitively in his novel *62: Modelo para armar*. His figures illustrate relationships and coincidences between events that seem to have no logical connection at all.

In "El otro cielo," places, characters, events and epochs intermingle in a story narrated by a young Argentinean. He lives in Buenos Aires, works in the Stock Exchange, and is engaged to marry Irma. Since adolescence, however, he has been capable of transporting himself psychically and physically to Paris. As he walks through the Güemes Arcade in Buenos Aires during the decades before Perón was elected president for the first time the smells and sounds provide a bridge for him to cross over to the arcades of Paris during the 1870's.

The narrative flows freely and continuously back and forth, even within sentences, between two worlds. The narrator inhabits both at will: Buenos Aires under the threat of increasing militarism and World War II, and Paris menaced by a strangler named Laurent and a Prussian invasion. The young man escapes from a rigidly routinized life with his mother and his fiancée, Irma. He enters another world in which there is the unfettered love of the prostitute Josiane, the mysterious young South American stranger who frequents the same bars, and the strangler Laurent who roams the neighborhood.

His passage to the "the other heaven," however, becomes more difficult for him as the story progresses. The terror that grips the inhabitants of the Parisian district begins to usurp the charm of the protagonist's adventures into Josiane's life. During a last visit to Paris, he learns of Laurent's—alias Paul the Marseillais—capture and the South American's death in his hotel room. He intuitively suspects a relationship between the two men:

And out of all that, I separated, like one who pulls two dry flowers off a garland, the two deaths which somehow seemed in my eyes symmetrical, the South American's and Laurent's, the one in his hotel room, the other dissolving into nothingness to yield his place to Paul the Marseillais, and they were almost the same death, something erased forever in the neighborhood's memory.[28]

After the two deaths, the protagonist returns to Buenos Aires where his marriage to Irma and his family obligations impede his escapes to Paris. Actually, however, the link to "the other heaven" has been mysteriously broken by the absence of Laurent and the South American:

Some days I get to thinking about the South American, and in that half-hearted ruminating I invent a sort of consolation, as if he had killed Laurent and myself with his own death; sensibly I tell myself no, I'm exaggerating, any day now I'll again venture into the gallery district and find Josiane surprised by my long absence. And between one thing and another I stay home drinking mate, listening to Irma, who's expecting in December, and wonder, not too enthusiastically, if at election time I'll vote for Perón or for Tamborini, if I'll vote none of the above and simply stay home drinking mate and looking at Irma and the plants in the patio.[29]

As in the novel *Rayuela*, Cortázar's Argentinean protagonist finally returns to his native land. Although the Paris of "El otro cielo" and of *Rayuela* is appealing and adventurous, allowing both protagonists a seemingly unfettered existence, they both seem to recognize the impending problems in their own countries. There is eventually no escape from one's national reality and life's routines no matter how far one manages to travel, psychically or physically.

The key to the mysterious relationship, the constellation or "figure," formed by Laurent, the South American, the protagonist, and even the author Cortázar, lies in an analysis of the two epigraphs which appear in the story. Both quotes are from *Les Chants de Maldoror*, published in Paris in 1868, by Isidore Ducasse, the Count of Lautréamont. "Those eyes don't belong to you . . . Where did you get them?," queries Maldoror, the protagonist of the narrative poem, as he confronts a shadow in his room. It turns out to be his own image in a mirror. The second quote reflects Maldoror's longing for the prostitutes of the district: "Where have the gaslights gone? What has become of the vendors of love?" Both epigraphs are applicable to the Argentinean of "El otro cielo." He sees his image reflected as a double who walks among the prostitutes of the Galerie Vivienne in Paris.

A series of parallels also exist between *Les Chants de Maldoror* and its author Lautréamont, and "El otro cielo" and its author Cortázar. *Les Chants de Maldoror* depicts man's bestiality and his lack of greatness, seeing him as a being not at all superior to animals. It emphasizes gratuitous brutality, violence, and sexual perversions. Although not to the same degree, "El otro cielo" evokes the violence of a roaming strangler, a guillotine scene, and hints of a sexually perverse South American.

Two characters in "El otro cielo" are mirror images or doubles of the real Count of Lautréamont,

Isidore Ducasse. The name of the story's strangler Laurent is a shortened version of Lautréamont, which emphasizes the accented letters. The story's young South American living in Paris around 1860, also has a name that sounds French. Like the fictitious South American, the real Count of Lautréamont was a writer living in Paris. His book *Les Chants de Maldoror* evokes the same horror as that created by the strangler Laurent in "El otro cielo."

Cortázar is also part of the Laurent-South American-Lautréamont-Argentinean "figure." Cortázar, born in Belgium of Argentinean parents in 1914, lived in Argentina and has for more than twenty years now resided in Paris where he writes in Spanish. Isidore Ducasse, born of French parents in Montevideo, Uruguay, in 1846, lived both in Latin America and in Paris where he wrote in French. He died there in 1870 at a young age. Cortázar's biography, therefore, partially reflects Lautréamont's, somewhat in reverse, as in a mirror image. Cortázar, too, is fascinated by man's bestiality, his sexual perversions, as well as eroticism and violence.

In the story, therefore, when Laurent is captured, and the young South American writer dies, the protagonist sees his place in the constellation fade. He attained glimpses of his reflection in two characters in many ways symbolic of Lautréamont in a Paris of 1970. Similarly, Cortázar seems to intuit his place in a figure which links himself in his circumstance to Isidore Ducasse, the Count of Lautréamont.

Upon reading the manuscript of this study, Cortázar wrote me the following explanation in order to emphasize the strangely fascinating relationship between the protagonist, the mysterious South American, and the strangler of his short story and the true life Lautréamont:

The South American who shows up at times in bars and who later dies in a hotel room *is* Lautréamont in person. All the details prove it for whoever is familiar with the little we know about the Count: his physical features—tall, very young, pale, with sloped shoulders—and his death, they know what the hotel room looked like and I followed that description.

Besides, Lautréamont lived in the Stock Exchange district during the period depicted in the short story. The vague idea that the protagonist intuits at the end of the story is that the South American proves that he, the narrator, and Laurent, the murderer, are mere mental projections of Lautréamont. When the South American (Lautréamont) dies, Laurent is caught—therefore he will disappear at the same time—and the narrator "dies," as far as his life in Paris is concerned, since he can no longer return and must conform to his mediocre life in Buenos Aires.

Of course, none of this is logical, but that's not something I have to explain to you who know me so well. It simply seemed to me that perhaps the reader might not understand my interpretation of the story.

2

Figures, Searches, and Centers

Juan, Horacio and Andrés, if you put the three of them together, I think you actually have me.

—*Julio Cortázar*

For Cortázar the short story exacts a high degree of perfection, a precise language without excess vocabulary, a decisive approach. Cortázar explained the difference between his concept of the short story and of the novel as follows:

> The novel allows for bifurcations, development, digressions. Curiously, the novel is a much more dangerous genre than the short story because it permits all kinds of liberties, of carelessness. You let yourself go writing a novel. You have to be very careful later in the final draft.

Although Cortázar alters his short stories very little —"There's something that makes them almost perfect while I'm writing"; the novels require more revisions. "With the novels I have thrown out many chapters that seemed important to me at the moment but that later, after reading the entire book, were repetitive or useless or might have distracted the reader." Nevertheless as he explained, the technique of writing has not been difficult for him for a long time now:

> I think that after twenty or thirty years of writing, the technical aspects of my work are solved. I have a certain capacity, let's call it a rhythmical capacity, that allows me to develop the different episodes and to know pretty much where and how they ought to end and how they should be joined one to another. That's not hard for me. What is difficult is exploring the depths of each situation that I'm relating as profoundly as possible. But the technical "smoothness," the development of the book, is not difficult for me now.

Cortázar admitted, however, that the beginnings of his novels, are a problem; whereas "the endings write themselves." He noted that with his novels he feels obliged by a sudden anguish to finish them quickly. "I wrote the end of *Rayuela*, the last chapters in the insane asylum, in forty-eight hours, and that time in almost an hallucinatory state." However, his experience with the beginning of *Rayuela* was quite different. He wrote the episode in which Talita is perched on the planks suspended between two windows high above the street—a chapter in the second half of the book—well before he even knew the episode would develop into the novel. And he started *62: Modelo para armar* three times.

Cortázar agreed with the critics in their estimation that *Rayuela*, his second novel, is his best. He qualified the statement however, by adding that critics and he, too, might well be of a different opinion ten years from now. Nevertheless, casting false modesty aside, he asserted—as do the critics—that that novel has

> profoundly influenced a good deal of Latin American fiction in the last ten years. There has been an enormous yet dual impact of *Rayuela* on the young people who began to write at that time. The negative repercussion is imitation, as was the case with the imitators of Borges. Many little "hopscotchs" have been published, consciously or unconsciously, all over the place, utilizing the same techniques of inserting quotes, of the open ended story and of hopscotch-like characters. Usually most of that is mediocre. But, on the other hand, there has been another type of influence, a kind of liberation from prejudices and from taboos in the realm of language. . . . *Rayuela* has contributed to making people take off their ties in order to write.

Cortázar emphasizes his identification with a particular character in his novels, especially with Horacio Oliveira of *Rayuela*, Juan of *62: Modelo para armar* and Andrés of *Libro de Manuel*. He notes that these men, great seekers of a new way of life, of love, and a more just social order, always failed even though they never lost hope.

Don't forget that an author usually attributes to some characters in his books the realization of his own desires, his own dreams. There are two ways of doing it. One is that those people attain the author's dreams, a vicarious way of acquiring what one wants by means of a character. In my case my characters habitually fail in the search for their dreams and their ideals even though they never lose hope. They're optimists, as I am. I think it's the honest approach. It's too easy to make a character be all that you are not. I think that when my characters represent me a little, they are what I am. They usually go a bit beyond, perhaps accomplish a little more than I in some ways but there is definitely not a great deal of difference between us. They end up being almost as they always were.

Today I would be incapable of writing a book like *The Winners*. I lack the innocence to do it.
—*Julio Cortázar*

Los premios (The Winners)

Julio Cortázar began writing his first novel, published in 1960, during a long boat trip. Recalling that time Cortázar noted: "I was very happy writing it." He wanted to see if he could handle a large number of characters, eighteen, something which he had never done before in his short stories.

Los premios is about a voyage, an unexpectedly short cruise aboard a mysterious ship, the *Malcolm.* Following the directions they have received from the office of Municipal Affairs, a group of Argentineans gather at the London Café in Buenos Aires. They, and their guests, are winners of a government lottery. The prize is a cruise of uncertain destination and indefinite duration.

That night, the winners are mysteriously transported by bus to the ship. Once aboard they form acquaintances according to cultural interests. The conversations are as varied as the individuals themselves, touching on love, literature, metaphysics, and ordinary gossip. Some passengers engage in harmonious relationships, others in hostile confrontations. Love is present in all of its ramifications from inhibited sexuality and sensual eroticism to profound friendships and homosexual encounters.

The mysterious atmosphere on board becomes more evident when the passengers try to make contact with the officers. The crew speaks a strange language; the passengers are denied knowledge of the ship's itinerary; they cannot locate the boat's doctor; and they are forbidden access to the stern of the ship. Finally the passengers are informed that a rare form of typhus has broken out among the crew. The *Malcolm* is anchored off shore at Quilmes, a very short distance away from Buenos Aires.

The passengers divide into two groups: those who accept the official explanation of a possible epidemic and those who decide to uncover the mystery behind what they consider to be a lie. In groups the challengers descend into the lower labyrinthine passages of the ship searching unsuccessfully for an access route to the stern and for clues to the uncomfortable secrecy surrounding the voyage.

When the young boy Jorge becomes ill, a few of the passengers led by Gabriel Medrano force their way to the stern in order to cable ashore for help. The victorious arrival at this jealously guarded region of the ship is immediately transformed into a personal defeat for Medrano. A sailor shoots him as he breaks into the radio room, and he dies. His body is mysteriously removed from the ship.

After an immobilized cruise of three days, the passengers are once more gathered together. They are to be transfered by hydroplane from the *Malcolm* to Buenos Aires. The Inspector offers his regrets for a lamentable voyage. The official is careful to note, however, that the outbreak of typhus necessitated an imposed discipline to protect the health of the passengers. He describes the "imprudence of the victim, who illegally crossed the precautionary sanitary barrier and reached the contaminated zone." The official urges the passengers to sign declarations so that false rumors about the incident will not spread. Most of the passengers choose to sign the false statement, to ignore the senseless killing, and to believe the unlikely alibi given by the officials. Paula, Raul, López, Claudia, Persio, and Atilio, however, refuse to sign. The voyage comes to an end as the passengers disperse.

In the epigraph to the novel, Cortázar cites a passage from Dostoyevsky's *The Idiot*:

What is an author to do with ordinary people, absolutely "ordinary," and how can he put them before his readers so as to make them at all interesting? It is impossible to leave them out of fiction altogether, for commonplace people are at every moment the chief and essential links in the chain of human affairs; if we leave them out, we lose all semblance of truth.[1]

Among the winners Cortázar included a cross-section of Buenos Aires society, though he insists that this was not intentional. Paula Lavalle is aboard at the invitation of the architect Raul Costa. They are both part of a wealthy, bored, and cynical generation, always in search of adventures to escape from mundane life. Paula is a sensual redhead who begins a friendship with Carlos López. Raul is a homosexual intent upon seducing an adolescent Felipe Trejo.

Carlos López and Dr. Restelli are middle-class schoolteachers. The latter is an advocate of law and order. Somewhat of a class snob, he exhibits an affected language and mannerism. López, on the other hand is a liberal, a tango lover, and a skeptic who joins the rebellious group.

The middle class is also represented by Claudia Lewbaum, her son Jorge, and Gabriel Medrano. Claudia, who is divorced, is an attentive mother. She has invited an old family friend, Persio, to travel with them. With Medrano, she forms a profound relationship which is prematurely terminated by his death. Her son Jorge is a child with a playful imagination who creates exotic and symbolic words to characterize the crew. His neologisms—antmen, glucids, and lipids—echo the sounds, albeit not the meaning, of Cortázar's creations in *Historias de cronopios y de famas*. Jorge's illness motivates the final assault on the radio room.

Gabriel Medrano, a dentist, uses the voyage as an excuse to break off with his present lover, Bettina. Although he is attracted to the sincere and intelligent Claudia, he has nightmares about Bettina. Because of his soul searching, Medrano is chosen by Cortázar as the sacrificial victim during the attack on the stern. "Medrano's death hurt me a lot," confessed Cortázar alluding sympathetically to this character.

The Trejo family and Nora and Lucio are representatives of the lower middle class. The Trejos seem to move about the ship in a group constantly bickering with each other. They behave condescendingly to the lower-class Presutti family, trying in this way to establish a distance between them. Felipe Trejo, who won the trip with his lottery ticket, was forced to invite his parents and sister Beba on the voyage. Felipe, an adolescent with contradictory sexual propensities needs to assert his masculinity and independence. The voyage initiates him into homosexuality.

Nora and Lucio form a pathetic young couple. They, like the Trejo family, do not want to become involved with the rebels aboard. Nora has run away with Lucio without being married to him. Her middle-class mores haunt her every word and act. She is in constant fear of having her unmarried status exposed, and she is obsessed by sexual taboos in her relationship with her lover. Lucio is also basically self-centered and indifferent to the mysterious events aboard the *Malcolm*.

Atilio Presutti—nicknamed the Pelusa—his mother, his fiancée, and her mother complete the social spectrum. They represent the lower class from the Genoese quarter in Buenos Aires. The Pelusa, at the center of the group, is an extroverted and generous young man around whom the women revolve like satellites. He is uninhibited and genuine in his actions, joining the rebellious forces as he intuits their just cause. He becomes one of the most sympathetically portrayed characters, as Cortázar himself pointed out in an author's note at the end of the novel: "Who would have told me that the Pelusa, who wasn't one of my favorites would assume such great stature at the end?"

Perhaps the most significant feature of the character development in *Los premios* is Cortázar's deft handling of a large cast. Each social group has its own realistic manner of conversation—allowing for personal differences, as well—which ranges from literary dilletantism to low-class jargon. Cortázar skillfully weaves the destinies together revealing just enough of their personalities, grandeur and weakness, to effect magnetic attractions and rejections between individuals.

Among the characters, such as Don Galo—an old Galician millionaire confined to a wheel chair—Claudia Lewbaum's friend Persio achieves a special role in the novel. For it is he who tries to analyze and abstract the meaning behind the aleatory encounters of individuals aboard the *Malcolm*. By profession he is a corrector of proofs at a publishing house. Aboard the *Malcolm* however, he is a "voyeur," a medium whose words—poetic, prophetic, and metaphysical—grope to decipher the "figure" formed by a chance meeting of the winners.

There are two phenomena in *Los premios*, both related to the character of Persio, that appear again in altered forms in some of Cortázar's other novels: the author's intervention in the fiction and an unusual novelistic structure. The external structure of *Los premios* is comprised of a prologue, three chapters designated as First, Second, and Third Day, and an epilogue. Within those divisions are nine sections preceded by letters A to I, and set in italicized print. In these alphabetized passages, Cortázar breaks with the novelesque form. He enters into the fiction by means of first and third person narrative to observe and interpret Persio's thoughts. Persio is, therefore, a vehicle, a voice for the author's observations concerning the events aboard the *Malcolm.*

The monologues are the key to the external action. They synthesize, in a bird's eye view, the passengers' individual soul searching which takes place during the voyage. Although many critics found the monologues to be aesthetic digressions which interfere with the main plot and seem to have been added afterwards, Cortázar maintains that they were written exactly where they appear in the novel.

Persio's monologues are exceptional in *Los premios* not only because they cause a rupture in the novelistic plot but also because of their poetic nature. In opposition to the logical, realistic, conversational prose of the major part of the novel, the monologues are a beautiful rendering of analogical prose. In these passages especially the first monologues, Cortázar comes as close as he ever will to a surrealist automatic writing based on subconscious associations, on free flowing analogies, and on strangely provocative imagery. "I felt a necessity to pass over into another kind of language," he notes. At the time, he decided to write the monologues somewhat as the Frenchman Raymond Roussel had composed his books, based on assonance and phonetic resonance, allowing himself to be carried along by the rhythm of the words. "If you reread the first ten lines of Persio's first monologue, you'll discover an internal rhythm that flows from one sentence to another . . . but that lasted for only a short time . . ."

The following passage is from Persio's fifth monologue. He is trying to fathom the vision of the ship as a guitar:

He has heard the guitar of the ship's cables resound weakly, the gigantic fingernail of space scratches out its first sound, almost immediately drowned out by the vulgarity of the waves and the wind. A damnable sea, because of its monotony and poverty, an immense, gelatinous green cow girding the ship which violates it persistently, in an endless battle between the iron penis and the viscous vulva, which shudders at every towering of spume. Momentarily above the inane and common copulation, the guitar of space flings down its exasperating call to Persio. Uncertain of what he has heard, his eyes closed, Persio knows that only the stammered vocabulary, the hesitant luxury of the largest words, loaded down like eagles with their royal prisoners, will, in the end, answer to his inmost self, his deepest feelings of his inner being and comprehension, the intolerable resonance of the strings. Fearful and small, moving like a fly over immeasurable surfaces, the mind and lips feel hesitantly the mouth of the night, the fingernail of space, and the pale hands of the mosaic maker piece in the fragments of blue, gold, and beetleback green in the too tenuous outlines of this musical drawing which is taking form. Suddenly a word, a well-rounded and heavy noun (but the brick doesn't always stick in the mortar) halfway constructed, collapses with a snail's scream lost in the flames. Persio lowers his head and stops understanding, he no longer even understands that he has stopped understanding.[2]

Persio's vision of the boat is described as having the shape of a guitar created by Picasso in a painting owned by the French poet Guillaume Apollinaire. Interestingly enough, this image conjures up many possible meanings: a cubist painting's multiplicity of fragmented perspectives in a spatial arrangement similar to the labyrinthine interactions of the passengers or the compartments of the ship; or a poet's magical vision of reality, like that of Apollinaire's own Persio, the magus in his first poetical work, *L'Enchanteur pourrissant* (The Rotting Enchanter).

In these monologues, Persio is situated somewhere in between heaven and earth. Like an astrologer he observes the stars above, but he also views the people below as components of a great constellation, a figure, which they as individuals ignore. Persio sees the voyage as a chess game: "Every move is a battle at sea, every step a river of words or tears, every square on the chess board a grain of sand, a sea of blood, a comedy of squirrels, or a farce given by buffoons who wander through fields of bells and applause."

Railing against false tradition and everyday triviality, he yearns to touch bottom, to experience oneness with the essence of a meaningful existence. But how to shout this to the Argentina that ignores him? He feels an irrational hope that he calls a "third hand," which ought to deliver his countrymen from the falseness that they live: an emptiness which they accept like the imposed lie of typhus on the *Malcolm* that confines them where the authorities wish.

Hidden within the dazzling analogical prose of Persio's monologues, concealed under metaphysical abstractions, is Persio's commentary on Argentinean reality—society's fearful acceptance of a falsely hollow order imposed upon it. He derides a South American reality steeped in everyday gestures in a dreamless present. "We stubbornly refuse to assume, as one must, a destiny in time."

Like the majority of the passengers aboard the *Malcolm*, Argentinean society, he suggests, maintains an attitude of "don't-get-involved-if-there-isn't-something-in-it-for-you." Persio helplessly watches the passengers play out their fate, "the dance of the wooden dolls, the first act of the American destiny . . . a dance of death . . ." He cries. Inciting man to rebel against a falsely imposed order, Persio recalls that Medrano is dead. He was the only one who in an act of rebellion actually reached the stern.

In the author's note, Cortázar denied that he wrote *Los premios* as an allegory. The result, nevertheless, is the same. *Los premios* can be interpreted on at least three significant levels. It is a thriller about a group of individuals who react in diverse ways when confronted by a closed and mysterious order. It is a metaphysical rendering of man in search of a forbidden absolute—the stern—the key to life's mystery. And it is an interpretation of a national reality—a complacent and indifferent Argentinean society that lived in the present without forging its own destiny.

Now ten years later, if I had to take along only
one of my books to a desert island,
I'd take *Rayuela.*
—*Julio Cortázar*

Rayuela (Hopscotch)

To describe Julio Cortázar's *Rayuela* would require either one word—brilliant—or at least 636 pages—one more than in the original Spanish version of the novel. Published in 1963, *Rayuela* has been reprinted more than a dozen times. It was considered by the London *Times Supplement* to be the "first great novel of Spanish America." In 1967, one year after it was published in English in the United States, *Hopscotch* won a National Book Award.

Although not "easy" reading, Cortázar's second novel is a rewarding and unique adventure. Like the children's game of chance for which it is named, *Rayuela* required patience and, above all, the reader's willingness to play, to actively participate in and follow the rules of the game that is the novel. The game, however, is unusual. It has a double playing board: two separate although related stories.

In an interview Cortázar denied that he expected us to read two novels in one. Nevertheless, he teases us to do so in the "Table of Instructions" to *Rayuela*, where he states that "this book consists of many books, but two books above all." The first book is read from Chapters 1 to 56. It is divided into two sections entitled "Del Lado de Allá" ("From the Other Side") and "Del Lado de Acá" ("From This Side"). After finishing Chapter 56, Cortázar advises the reader that he may ignore the rest of the book "with a clear conscience." However, once having reached the three stars indicating *The End* of Chapter 56, the reader, his gaming instinct piqued, will jump into book number two. The second book begins with Chapter 73 and follows a sequence of chapters in hopscotch fashion incorporating all but one from the first two sections and those of the third section entitled "De Otros Lados" ("From Diverse Sides"), subtitled "Expendable Chapters."

This double, and even multiple, novel is one of the reasons for the book's fame. It is considered to be a revolutionary view and structure of the novel in contemporary times. It contains a double trajectory: the story of man's self-analysis and a reevaluation of the traditional novel, its destruction and plan for rejuvenation. The two searches are intimately related. Oliveira, the protagonist of the traditionally read first book, seeks a *more authentic* basis for life: through the main character of the second book—the novel itself—Cortázar searches for a *more authentic* form of communication for Oliveira's anguished quest.

The first novel opens with Horacio Oliveira, an Argentinean intellectual living in Paris. It is around 1950 and he is about forty years old. Jobless, he spends his hours in continual self-analysis, questioning his every thought, word, action, and emotion. Therein lies his anguish. A product of rational Western civilization, he "over-thinks," drowning himself in a sea of dialectic possibilities.

Oliveira and his bohemian friends often gather for what they call the Serpent Club. Among the members are Ossip Gregorovius, who is a Russian intellectual, a

North American couple Babs and Ronald, two Frenchmen Étienne and Guy, the Chinese Wong and the Spaniard Perico. In smoke-filled rooms, they listen to jazz and converse about literature, music, philosophy and art.

The story begins with Horacio asking himself "Would I find La Maga?" La Maga is an Uruguayan woman living in Paris with her baby Rocamadour. Unlike her lover Horacio, she is spontaneous and intuitive. La Maga walks the streets of Paris like a child, searching for interesting objects and pieces of cloth. Oliveira finds her incapable of comprehending abstract ideas, the same ideas that bind him to reason. He envies her unfettered aleatory existence; and so like her, he wanders through Paris looking for unexpected adventures.

Oliveira, dissatisfied with his mundane, logical, self-centered life, tries to involve himself in unusual experiences. His refusal to behave in a conventionally sympathetic manner when Rocamadour dies, leads to a definitive break with La Maga. On another occasion he forces himself to listen to an absurdly horrendous piano recital and to sympathize with the grotesque pianist Berthe Trepat. During one of his adventures, he sinks to the depths of filth and misery while making love to a tramp under a bridge in Paris. This last episode results in his deportation to Buenos Aires.

In the second half of the first story, "From This Side," Oliveira continues to pursue his desire to become one with the universe, to rid himself of an existence stinking with trivia and logic. He is welcomed home to Buenos Aires by a devoted lover, Gekrepten, and by a childhood friend Traveler and his wife, Talita. Ironically Traveler has never journeyed far from where they work. A triangle forms as Horacio confuses the lost La Maga with Talita and is attracted to her. He also senses that Traveler is his "double" the other side of the same coin—akin in spirit but different and complementary. He is what Oliveira could have been: an Argentinean without intellectual and existential anguish, at home in his own territory.

When the circus owner buys a sanatorium, the three move in to work among the crazy people. After kissing Talita one night in the sanatorium's morgue, Oliveira develops a persecution complex. Thinking that Traveler is trying to kill him, he locks himself in his room and constructs an intricate system of threads criss-crossed through the room like a spider web. He places basins and spitoons of water and ball bearings on the floor and sits in the dark on the sill by the open window waiting for Traveler to enter. Traveler falls into the trap. Cursing at the obstructions, he makes his way through the threads to a chair, sits down, and talks to Horacio. Outside, three stories down, Talita and the others gather in the yard near a hopscotch design and watch Oliveira lean dangerously out the window. Even though he refuses to leave the room with Traveler, Oliveira realizes that Traveler is really his friend. The story ends when Traveler returns to Talita below. From the open window Horacio watches the couple standing in the hopscotch design. He thinks of how easy it would be to let himself fall out into the hopscotch.

The author never tells us whether or not Horacio commits suicide or goes crazy. When read for the second time, following Cortázar's designated scheme, Chapter 56 described above is followed by seven more chapters. The story then "terminates"—an unfair word as Cortázar would say—with two chapters that continue alternating eternally, 58-131-58-131-. The mystery is not solved in those two chapters either. There a mixture of events and conversations takes place as if they were whirring through Oliveira's head in a confused timeless state of dream-wakefulness: Talita is in the sanitorium and Gekrepten is in her apartment but both are putting compresses on Horacio's brow; Traveler is giving him injections to calm him down; the voices of others in the sanatorium are commenting on Oliveira's adventure; Gekrepten is pattering on about trivia and food; and Horacio is talking to Traveler about entering an order of monks who combat spiritual ills. Is he recovering from a fall or has he gone crazy?

Horacio Oliveira is the focal point of *Rayuela.* The other characters serve to explain him. The Serpent Club forms a background for several dialectical conversations and an atmosphere of bohemia that surrounds the protagonist. However, any of the characters that are even somewhat developed, and most are not, are but shadows of Oliveira's possibilities: Traveler—fragments of what he'd like to be; La Maga—mirror image of his intellectual self; Gregorovius. They all complement him.

Oliveira is not content with life. He is a prisoner of reason who admits that the true crises in life cannot be solved by logic. He realizes that intellectual meditation falsifies reality for him and so he must renounce reason. Yet he cannot so easily dismiss the sediment of Western culture. Oliveira tries to destroy reason with his intelligence, a kind of intellectual suicide as Étienne describes it: "The scorpion stabbing itself in the neck, tired of being a scorpion but having to have recourse to its own scorpioness in order to do away with itself as a scorpion."

Even his emotions are controlled by an insatiable obsession with analysis. Oliveira abhors habitual responses, false sorrow, a love that becomes empty ritual. Yet in his relationship with La Maga, Oliveira is incapable of pure emotions. La Maga tells him that he does not know how to cry. Oliveira feels that love may be the answer to his search but he also fears that love may stagnate, and so he destroys it: "Maybe love was the highest enrichment, a giver of being; but only by bungling it could one avoid its boomerang effect . . ."

During one of the meetings of the Serpent Club, the members seated in the dark room carry on esoteric conversations while listening to jazz. La Maga's baby is sick but seems to be sleeping quietly despite the noise from within the apartment, the banging of an irate neighbor above, and the argument in the hallway.

Oliveira notices that Rocamadour is dead. His reaction is a denial of instinctual sorrow: "Fall into the pattern . . . Shout, turn on the light, start the obligatory hustle and bustle. Why? . . . Why turn on the light and shout if it won't do any good?" He informs the others secretly without letting La Maga know. Much later, when she approaches the child to give him some medicine, she discovers that he is dead. As the others reach for a cologne handkerchief to revive her and to cover her eyes, Oliveira, apart from the group jokes to himself, "If that's cologne they're going to blind her." Rather than act the-way-that-he-should, Oliveira laughs about the tragic consequences of Rocamadour's death. Laughter and irony at the expense of another's tragedy is clearly black humor: a release valve for emotions that do not know how to express themselves.

Oliveira continually wavers between becoming involved with people and politics, or remaining an aloof observer. Here, too, his intellectual dialectics render him immobile. He feels that every act entails the admission of a lack "of something not yet done and which could have been done . . . It was better to withdraw, because withdrawl from action was the protest itself and not its mask." La Maga maintains that Oliveira could never be a hero, a saint or a perfect escapist. She tells him, "You think too much before you do anything."

To Oliveira daily life governed by rules without exceptions is absurd. To waken every morning next to the same woman is as annoying to him as the certainty that the sun will rise in the east. Man, expelled from Eden, he says, was actually condemned to "bovine conformity, the cheap and dirty joy of work, and sweat of the brow and paid vacations."

Unable to accept existence as it is, Oliveira embarks upon a search for a new meaning to life. He must start anew, discard the ballast of Western traditional thought, actions, and habit; throw it out a window, and if necessary, himself with it—as he says. Like the cronopios he seeks to gain access to a more authentic albeit impractical and illogical realm. His search for the most part, however, is not joyous, like that of the cronopios', but anguished and solitary. Its symbol is the hopscotch game. Oliveira explains:

Hopscotch is played with a pebble that you move with the tip of your toe. The things you need: a sidewalk, a pebble, a toe, and a pretty chalk drawing, preferably in colors.

On top is Heaven, on the bottom is Earth, it's very hard to get the pebble up to Heaven, you almost always miscalculate and the stone goes off the drawing. But little by little you start to get the knack of how to jump over the different squares (spiral hopscotch, rectangular hopscotch, fantasy hopscotch, not played very often) and then one day you learn how to leave Earth and make the pebble climb up into Heaven . . . the worst part of it is that precisely at that moment, when practically no one has learned how to make the pebble climb up into Heaven, childhood is over all of a sudden and you're into novels, into the anguish of the senseless divine trajectory, into the speculation about another Heaven that you have to learn to reach too.[3]

In *Homo Ludens: A Study of the Play Element in Culture*, Johan Huizinga discusses the relationship between games and religion: "The turf, the tennis court, the chess board and the pavement hopscotch cannot formally be distinguished from the temple or the magic circle."[4] Cortázar uses the hopscotch in this ritualistic sense, as the symbol of a serious mystical search for an Absolute. To Cortázar the hopscotch resembles the mandala of Tibetan and other Far East religions. Composed of many compartments, the mandala is used for spiritual exercises and meditation. Cortázar maintains that the children's hopscotch also stems from religious origins, especially the type played in Argentina and in France for it has sections marked Heaven and Earth at opposite ends of the design. Cortázar has always been fascinated by that labyrinthine and ritualistic game.

The Heaven that Oliveira aims for is not the Christian Heaven. It is attainable in this lifetime. As in the hopscotch design, Heaven is on the same level as

Earth on the dirty sidewalk. One must play the game in order to reach it during one's existence on earth.

Heaven or the Absolute, as Oliveira explains to La Maga, is "that moment in which something attains its maximum depth, its maximum reach, its maximum sense, and becomes completely uninteresting." It is never eternally attainable for once possessed it ceases to be the Absolute. It is a point at which contradictions, the infernal dialectic that obsesses Oliveira, fuse—black and white, night and day, laughter and tears, dream and vigil. Oliveira describes the Absolute metaphorically, "We ought to invent the sweet slap, the bee-kick. But in this world ultimate syntheses are yet to be discovered."

The Absolute, or Center, as Oliveira names it, is a total encounter with self and surrounding circumstance achieved without reason. The Center is reached by desire, imagination and adventure. It has many names but above all it is a "kibbutz of desire."

> Kibbutz; colony, settlement, taking root, the chosen place in which to raise the final tent, where you can walk out into the night and have your face washed by time, and join up with the world, with the Great Madness, with the Grand Stupidity, lay yourself bare to the crystallization of desire, of the meeting . . . Kibbutz of desire, not of the soul, not of the spirit. And even though desire might also be a rough definition of incomprehensible forces, he could feel it present and at work, present in every mistake and also in every forward leap, that was being a man, not just a body and a soul but that inseparable totality, that ceaseless meeting up with lacks, with everything they had stolen from the poet, the vehement nostalgia for a land where life could be babbled out according to other compasses and other names.[5]

In order to attain glimpses of the Center, Oliveira embarks upon his initiatory journey. To encompass reality from all perspectives, all dialectical possibilities, he must seek ubiquity. Ridding himself of solely subjective feelings, Oliveira attempts to experience "otherness." He realizes, however, that in order to participate in the feelings of another he must first descend into himself. Even then the "other" must be disposed to communicate with him.

> "*Underneath it all* we could be what we are on the surface," Oliveira thought, "but we would have to live in a different way. And what does it mean to live in a different way? Maybe to live absurdly in order to do away with the absurd, to dive into one's self with such force that the leap will end up in the arms of someone else. Yes, maybe love, but that *otherness* lasts only as long as a woman lasts, and besides only as everything concerns that woman. Basically there is no such thing as otherness, maybe just that pleasant thing called *togetherness*. Of course, that is something . . ." Love, an ontologizing ceremony, a giver of being. And that is why he was thinking only now of what he should have thought about in the beginning: without the possession of self, there was no possession of otherness, and who could really possess himself?[6]

Oliveira pursues adventures that force him to confront the absurd world that he feels surrounds him. He maintains that the only way to break out of this infinite absurdity is by living absurdly. Turning that thought over and over in his mind, Oliveira seeks refuge from a rainy Paris day by attending a piano concert by Madame Berthe Trepat. The pianist's grotesque appearance as she moves across the stage like a marionette is followed by an indescribably bad performance at the piano. Of the twenty people in the audience, only

Oliveira remains until the end. During the concert he feels a strange sympathy for the old woman who is "trying to present works in premiere, which in itself was a great thing in this world of the polonaise, the clair de lune, and the ritual fire dance." He forces himself not only to listen to the entire concert but also to congratulate her enthusiastically at the end. He comforts her as she cries over the indifference of the audience and the ungratefulness of Valentin, a friend who introduced her performance and then left. Oliveira offers to accompany her home.

Oliveira's emotions undergo a strange transformation as he walks through the streets of Paris with Berthe Trepat. Despite his external politeness, he is actually repulsed by the old woman with her delusions of grandeur and her grotesque appearance. The desire to vomit or to put her out of her misery wells up inside of him as they walk in the rain. He cannot believe that this sputtering old woman is grasping his arm; perhaps, he thinks, it is not actually he who accompanies her but his *doppelgänger*.

Strangely his disgust turns to joy as he undergoes a transformation:

He suddenly had a terrible urge to laugh (and it hurt his empty stomach, cramped his muscles, it was strange and painful and when he would tell Wong, about it he wouldn't begin to believe it). Not at Berthe Trepat, who was going on about the honors she had received in Montpellier and Pau, with an occasional reference to the gold medal. Nor at his having been stupid enough to volunteer his company. He wasn't quite sure where the urge to laugh was coming from, it came from something previous, something farther back, not because of the concert, which should have been the most laughable thing in the world. Joy, something like a physical form of joy. Even though it was hard for him to believe it, joy. He could have laughed with contentment, pure, delightful, inexplicable contentment. "I'm going crazy," he thought. "And with this nut on my arm, it must be contagious."[7]

Her patter about Valentin, the homosexual that lives with her, and his adventures, warms Oliveira. He feels momentarily saved from everything that had happened all day.

That inexplicable joy quickly disappears, however, when they approach her apartment building and she doesn't invite him in. Sensing that Valentin is locked inside with a boyfriend, Madame Trepat becomes uncontrollably agitated. Sincerely trying to help her, Oliveira offers to arrange for a hotel room. Ironically she interprets his generosity as an illicit proposal and slaps his face. Walking off in the rain Oliveira thinks about the absurd adventure. He had only hoped to prolong the joy, to sit down in Madame Trepat's apartment, to have a drink with her and Valentin, to warm his wet feet by the fire.

For a few moments he had divested himself of analytical, unfeeling Horacio Oliveira. Engaged in an absurd adventure, he touched bottom in himself and leapt out toward "the other":

He said to himself that he had not been such an idiot to have felt so happy seeing the old woman home. But that as always he had paid dearly for that foolish happiness. Now he would begin to reproach himself, put himself down little by little until the same old thing was left there, a hole where time was blowing, an imprecise continuum that had no set bounds.[8]

It is in brink situations, absurd adventures, "happenings," that Oliveira finds a glimpse of the Center, a bridge to another more provocative approach to life. These episodes are usually characterized by a strange mixture of pathos and humor. Cortázar feels that brink situations heighten the reader's interest, although he did lament their hypnotic effect for he did not intend to render the reader helpless and passive. Chapter 41 about Talita perched atop the wooden plank is a good illustration of the tension produced by such a totally illogical adventure.

Oliveira, seated at the window in his apartment in Buenos Aires is straightening out bent tacks. He shouts across the alley, a short distance away to Traveler's apartment asking him for some tacks and also for *yerba* to make *maté*. Rather than walk down three flights of stairs, across the alley and upstairs to Traveler's apartment to get the package of tea and tacks, Oliveira insists on devising a bridge to connect the buildings. With planks suspended between windows, Traveler and Oliveira watch each other closely as Talita, scantily clad in only a bathrobe, is chosen to crawl out onto the improvised bridge under the hot sun. The neighbors gather below to watch. As she slowly inches her way toward Oliveira's window, Talita senses that the men's conversation is really about her, as if they were carrying on a ritual, a trial by fire with her at the stake. Although Talita's life is in danger when Traveler leaves the window to fetch a hat for her, Oliveira and she begin to play a word game called seesaw questions.

During the acrobatics Gekrepten enters Oliveira's apartment. She is completely indifferent to the dangerous game being played between Traveler, Talita and Oliveira. Her idle chatter about dentists, milk, and dressmakers, forms a strangely ironic counterpoint to

Talita's and Oliveira's conversation: mundane trivia juxtaposed with serious conversation as the two men seem to psychically vie for Talita. Finally wearing the hat, Talita throws the package of *yerba* and tacks through Oliveira's window. Rather than crawl forward just a few feet to Oliveira's outstretched arms, she backs up slowly and returns to Traveler. The tension of this seemingly illogical adventure dissipates.

When Horacio opens the novel by asking himself if he'll find La Maga, he is posing a question which is a key to his search. For him she is a "frightful mirror"; they love each other "in a sort of dialectic of magnet and iron filings, attack and defense, handball and wall." This dialectic double, therefore, possesses all the qualities which Oliveira strives for: instead of an immobilizing logic and an abstract dialectic La Maga exhibits intuitive desire and a communion with the world in its concrete manifestations. She is adventurous and spontaneously wanders through Paris in search of objects with which she constructs mobiles and useless machines. She is quite obviously a cronopio. Oliveira's search for a Center is in part a search for his other side—La Maga. In order to perceive reality from a ubiquitous perspective, he has to apprehend that which he lacks—his double—his mirror image, which of course is always the reverse view of the person it reflects. La Maga, like a medium, participates magically in aspects of reality that Horacio gropes to experience dialectically:

> There are metaphysical rivers, she swims in them like that swallow swimming in the air, spinning madly around a belfry, letting herself drop so that she can rise up all the better with the swoop. I describe and define and desire those rivers, but she swims in them. And she doesn't know

it, any more than the swallow. It's not necessary to know things as I do, one can live in disorder without being held back by any sense of order. That disorder is her mysterious order, that bohemia of body and soul which opens its true doors wide for her. Her life is not disorder except for me, buried among the prejudices I despise and respect at the same time. Me, inexorably condemned to be pardoned by La Maga who judges me without knowing it. Oh, let me come in, let me see some day the way your eyes see.[9]

Through his love for her, Horacio hopes to gain the Center. He loves her because she is "from the other side" inviting him to jump. Tormented by her love because he cannot use it as a bridge, "a passport-love, a mountain-pass love, a key-love, a revolver-love, a love that will give him the thousand eyes of Argos, ubiquity . . ." Oliveira breaks up their relationship. Unable to deny his own image in favor of hers, he must either destroy her by bringing her to his side or escape. He walks out on her, rationalizing that it is better to separate before their love becomes an odious habit.

Nevertheless, Oliveira does not escape from La Maga. He sees her in many women, he supplants Talita with her image. In Chapter 56, Oliveira sees Talita-La Maga in the hopscotch beneath his window. He ponders the leap from his reasoned reality into La Maga's, into the Heaven on the hopscotch. During the second reading of the novel, it is subtly suggested that Oliveira will never take that final leap—to suicide, to madness, to a self-denial—for Cortázar states in Chapter 104 that life is "a *commentary* of something else we cannot reach which is there within reach of the leap we will not take."

This pathetic statement does not, however, mean that life is worthless, that Oliveira's anguished search is futile. For Oliveira's search is not a purely existential one. Existentialism places man in the center of an absurd world, saddles him with responsibility for his existence, and dares him to dignify the miseries of mankind during his lifetime. Existential man must bear his social and moral cosmos like Sisyphus condemned by the Greek gods, who chained him to a rock and forced him to eternally push the rock up the hill only to have it roll down again and again. Instead Oliveira tries, like the cronopios and La Maga, to destroy and enchant the rock, as André Breton, the magus of surrealism, proposed to do, by means of imagination and desire.

The existentialist lacked a sense of humor, Oliveira's principal weapon. It is precisely Cortázar's capacity for "pulling our leg" and for laughing at himself through Oliveira that saves his character from pure existential anguish. He explained his optimistic perspective in an interview:

> I detest solemn searches . . . What I like above all about the masters of Zen is their complete lack of solemnity. The deepest insights sometimes emerge from a joke, a gag, or a slap in the face. In *Rayuela* there's a great influence of that attitude, I might even say of that technique.[10]

Zen's method, surrealistic adventures, Jarry's pataphysics, all contribute to Cortázar's humor. "I've always thought humor is one of the most serious things there is,"[11] stated Cortázar in his inimitably contradictory manner.

In *Rayuela* humor is visible in all its forms. As Luis Harss and Barbara Dohmann pointed out, Cortázar employs gags, jokes, farce and fantasy. "His humor can be harsh, hectic, grotesque, ironic, jeering."[12] Even his manipulation of language, in jargon, slang, games and obscenity is humorous and imaginative. Some of the most successful "brink" scenes are replete with black humor.

Rayuela cannot be viewed as a novel about a pessimistic and futile search. Far from destroying logical man, Oliveira searches for a fusion of reason and desire, of opposites. He glimpses that union with Berthe Trepat and with Talita perched on the boards. Oliveira's optimism lies precisely in his search, the road, the voyage, the stone heading for Heaven. Morelli, a character in *Rayuela*, describes the importance of that game: "with each successive defeat there is an approach towards the final mutation, and . . . man only is in that he searches to be, plans to be, thumbing through words and modes of behavior and joy sprinkled with blood and other rhetorical pieces like this one."

When I told Cortázar that Oliveira could not possibly commit suicide by jumping out the window and that *Rayuela* is an essentially optimistic book—two conclusions which are not shared by all critics—Cortázar smiled and said:

> No, no, he doesn't jump. One doesn't know for sure: but he doesn't jump, no, no, I'm sure he doesn't jump. But there are critics, of course, who when they reviewed the book stated that at the end the protagonist commits suicide. Oliveira doesn't commit suicide. But I couldn't say that. It would have destroyed the book. The idea is that there you, or any other reader, have to decide. So, for example you decide, as I do, that Oliveira doesn't kill himself. But there are readers who decide that he does. Well, I feel sorry for them. It's too bad for them. The reader-accomplice has to decide. Of course it's an optimistic book.

Rayuela, read according to the plan set forth by

Cortázar in the "Table of Instructions," comprises at least 153 chapters. All of the original chapters, with the exception of Chapter 55, and ninety-eight new "Expendable Chapters," interspersed at random within the chronological sequence of the traditional story: 73-1-2-116-3-84-4-71-5-81-74-etc. The reader must piece together the collage of chapters, jumping through the book as if on a hopscotch board. In this way Cortázar exacts the reader's participation in constructing the second story.

Cortázar admits—by means of his spokesman Morelli—that this approach is destined for a limited audience, those who dare read the novel by means of an anti-novel scheme. For the "Expendable Chapters" often break the novelistic progression of the plot and comment on the actions and thoughts from another perspective. This second book is not for the "female-reader" (a term equally applicable to both sexes) who expects a ready-made story and dares not become involved in the action. It is for the "reader-accomplice," as Morelli explains:

> To attempt on the other hand a text that would not clutch the reader but which would oblige him to become an accomplice as it whispers to him underneath the conventional exposition other more esoteric directions. Demotic writing for the female-reader (who otherwise will not get beyond the first few pages, rudely lost and scandalized, cursing at what he paid for the book), with a vague reverse side of hieratic writing.[13]

Asked why he designated the unadventurous and passive reader as "female-reader" even though he applied the term to men as well, Cortázar quickly explained:

I ask pardon of the women of the world for the fact I used such a "machista" expression so typical of Latin American underdevelopment, and you should spell it out clearly in the interview. I did it innocently and I have no excuse. But when I began to hear the opinions of my friends, women readers who heartily insulted me, I realized that I had done something foolish. I should have put "passive-reader" and not "female reader" because there's no reason for believing that females are continually passive. They are in certain circumstances and are not in others, the same as males.

Some of the most important chapters dealing with Cortázar's theory of the anti-novel are included in the third section as notes from Morelli's manuscripts. Morelli, an old man who is a favorite author of the Serpent Club, appears in the traditional story also. There he is run over by a car and taken to the hospital. Ignorant of his identity, Oliveira observes the accident and decides to visit the convalescent. He discovers who he is and is entrusted with the keys to Morelli's apartment where the manuscript notes are filed. In this way the Cortázar-Morelli theory of the anti-novel finds its way into the "Expendable Chapters."

Cortázar-Morelli proposes to make the reader a "traveling companion" during the creative process of a new novel. The reader is very important to Morelli: "What I write ought to contribute to his mutation, displacement, alienation, transportation." By involving the reader in his workshop, making him juggle the chapters along with the author, Cortázar achieves a measure of complicity. His theory of the anti-novel, however, is applied even more daringly in his next novel *62: Modelo para armar*.

The "Expendable Chapters," then, comprise a

diary of the emerging novel, a heterogeneous collection of notes and meditations as well as excerpts from books and periodicals which parallel, echo, and contrast with the original chapters. Some of the additional chapters are only a few lines or paragraphs. As defensive explanations, quotes, theory and humor, they explain the gaps between adventures and conversations. Several of the excerpts are from literary sources by authors as diverse as Claude Levi-Strauss, Anais Nin, Malcolm Lowry, Achim Von Arnim, Antonin Artaud, and Georges Bataille.

The new sequence of chapters often creates an ironic echo. Such is the case with Chapter 130 which succeeds the death of Rocamadour. There *The Observer* in London warns about the "Perils of the Zipper," and the tragic consequences of a little boy catching his genitals in the zipper fly of his trousers. The fictitious scene of Rocamadour's death replete with "black" humor, is followed by a factual newspaper article equally as "black."

Cortázar's *Rayuela* is more than a metaphysical game of man's rebirth in life and a structural game which transforms the novel. It is also an author at play with his own language. Once again, the game is a ritual experience, a search for new modes of expression, a revival of language aimed at freeing it from outmoded and habitual molds.

Destroying literary rhetoric, doing away with traditional forms of writing, groping to express himself almost without words has always been a goal for Cortázar. Just as his character Oliveira would have liked to dispose of reason without the use of intelligence, Cortázar the author would like to "arrive at the word without words." But since that is an impossible task, he must be content with transforming language using it to rebel against its own mundane forms, just as Oliveira employs absurd adventures to survive in an absurd world. Cortázar does not oppose all language, only false, hollow, outmoded forms.

Cortázar's language acquires myriad tones: lyrical, comic, mystic, erotic, inventive, esoteric, ironic. He pokes fun at sacred expressions: "In the beginning was the copulative, to rape is to explain, but not always the other way around." Cortázar masters erotic descriptions as he equates jazz with sex:

> . . . and then the trumpet's flaming up, the yellow phallus breaking the air and having fun, coming forward and drawing back and towards the end three ascending notes, pure hypnotic gold, a perfect pause where all the swing of the world was beating in an intolerable instant, and then the supersharp ejaculation slipping and falling like a rocket in the sexual night . . .[14]

He also composes disarmingly tender prose, in Chapter 32 for example, in a letter written by La Maga to her dead baby Rocamadour:

> BABY Rocamadour, baby, baby. Rocamadour. By now I know you're like a mirror, Rocamadour, sleeping or looking at your feet. Here I am holding a mirror and thinking that it's you. But don't you believe it, I'm writing to you because you don't know how to read. If you did know I wouldn't be writing to you or I'd be writing about important things. Someday I'll have to write to you and tell you to behave and keep warm. Someday seems incredible, Rocamadour. Now I can only write to you in the mirror, sometimes I have to dry my finger because it gets wet with tears. . . . I've got my toes curled all the way under and I'm going to split open my shoes if I don't take them off,

and I love you so much, Rocamadour, baby Rocamadour, little garlic-clove, I love you so much, sugar-nose, sapling, toy pony . . .[15]

The imagery in *Rayuela* is rich in variety as well: plastic, impressionistic, poetic, expressionistic, surrealistic, and almost always unusual. At times the syntax is analogic, allowing thoughts to flow in a series of free associations. "A pureness as of coitus between crocodiles, not the pureness of oh Mary my mother with dirty feet; a pureness of a slate roof with doves who naturally shit on the heads of ladies wild with rage and radishes, a pureness of . . ."

The characters play with language. They invent games called seesaw-questions or cemetery games—the cemetery is a common dictionary, with dead words, of course. La Maga invents a language called Gliglish. It is based on sounds and neologisms which have no dictionary meaning but which, nevertheless allow the reader to glimpse their erotic intent:

> "Tell me how Ossip makes love," Oliveira whispered, putting his lips hard against La Maga's. . . .
>
> "He does it very well, longer."
>
> "But does he retilate your murt? Don't lie to me. Does he really retilate it?"
>
> "A lot. Everywhere, sometimes too much. It's a wonderful feeling."
>
> "And does he make you put your plinnies in between his argusts?"
>
> "Yes, and then we trewst our porcies until he says he's had enough, and I can't take it any more either, and we have to hurry up, you understand. But you wouldn't understand that, you always stay in the smallest gumphy."[16]

He makes unusual orthographic changes based on phonics in Chapter 69: "It waz a sad surprize to rede in the 'orthografik' the newz ov the demize in San Luis Potosi on march furst last of lootenant kernel (promoted to kernel on leving the surviss) Adolfo Abila Sanhes."

He joins words to emphasize their vulgarity: "The newsspreadlikewildfire." He has Oliveira interpolate an "h"—always silent in Spanish—in front of words to emphasize the absurdity of language and to cure himself of it. In English translation those passages employ a "wh":

He wrote, for example: "The great whaffair," or "the whintersection." It was enough to make him laugh and feel more up to preparing another mate. "Whunity," whrote Wholiveira. "The whego and the whother." He used this *wh* the way other people used penicillin.[17]

In Chapter 34, Cortázar alternates lines from his novel with those of a famous XIX Century Spanish novelist, Benito Pérez Galdós. He catches the reader off guard and emphasizes—as indicated in our italicized lines—his message. Oliveira is criticizing the worn out ideas and outmoded language of the classic Spanish novel that La Maga is reading:

uncle (in truth my father's first cousin), Don Rafael Bueno
after you swallow four or five pages you get in the groove
de Guzman y Ataide, wanted to put me up in his home; but I
and can't stop reading, a little like the way you can't help
demurred for fear of losing my independence. I was finally
sleeping or pissing, slavery or whipping or drooling. I was
able to effect a compromise between my comfortable freedom
finally able to effect a compromise, a style that uses prefabri-
and my uncle's gracious offer; and renting a flat in his build-
cated words to transmit superannuated ideas, coins that go

ing, I arranged matters so that I could be alone when I
from hand to hand, from generation to generation . . .[18]

The four epigraphs in *Rayuela* which introduce the novel and the first two sections are symbolic keys to the author's intent. The first excerpt is from an XVIII Century work entitled *Spirit of The Bible and Universal Morals, Drawn for the Old and New Testaments.* Cortázar's aspirations are echoed in that quote: "moved by the hope of being of particular help to youth." Ironically his contribution "to the reform of manners in general" differs greatly from the Christian ethic proposed in the religious text which like *Rayuela* is a "collection of maxims, counsels and precepts." Nevertheless, the same desire to reform humanity motivates both works.

Although Cortázar says that the book proposes no solutions and that he never has written with a didactic purpose in mind, he did recall the hundreds of letters he has received from youngsters who seem to identify with the novel. He wrote *Rayuela* for people of his own generation, but they hardly understood Oliveira's anguished search. On the other hand "The young people found there, their own questions, their daily anguish . . . They were not comfortable in the world, the world that belonged to their parents." *Rayuela* does not have to be didactic in order to accompany and comfort young people who see that the problems that they face are not theirs alone.

The second epigraph is a passage in mock-illiterate Argentine slang entitled *What I Would Like To Be If I Wasn't What I Am* by César Bruto. It is written in orthographically incorrect words. A dog, tired of his lowly life and filthy surroundings, dreams of being a swallow who can fly away to distant lands. He advises the reader, "I jes hope what I been writin down hear do somebody some good so he take a good look at how he livin and he dont be sorry when it too late and everythin is gone down the drain cause it his own fault." In this passage, Cortázar hints at his playful attitude toward language, his character's dejection and search for another country and life, and his admonition to us to evaluate our own lives before it's too late.

A third epigraph is written by Jacques Vaché, a friend of the French surrealist writer André Breton. Vaché was immortalized by the surrealists for his attitude of protest against traditionalism in society. One day he attended a premier performance of Guillaume Apollinaire's revolutionary play *The Breasts of Tiresias*. Vaché who considered this unusual play to be based on conventional and outmoded ideas, stood up, revolver in hand, and protested by firing it at random into the audience. Later Vaché committed suicide. A sentence quoted from his letter to André Breton precedes the first section of *Rayuela*: "Nothing kills a man like being forced to represent a country." Here Cortázar defends his character's internationalism—an Argentinean living in Paris—and, of course his own, since Cortázar himself has lived in France since 1951. Oliveira and Cortázar as well, carry their countries within themselves.

"From This Side" is prefaced by another quote by a Frenchman, this one from Apollinaire's *The Breasts of Tiresias*: "One must travel far to love one's home." Once again this epigraph has several levels of interpretation. Oliveira and Cortázar live far away from Argentina where they are able to view it from a more comprehensive perspective. Oliveira returns, Cortázar only visits. The epigraph can also symbolize Oliveira's personal search, his leaps into "otherness" in order to better understand himself.

Man's journey in search of a Center and Cortázar's revolutionary approach to the Latin American novel were perhaps subconsciously conceived during *Los premios*. They are born with *Rayuela*, and mature during his third novel *62: Modelo para armar*. While writing *Rayuela*, Cortázar was already projecting himself into another novel, another mode of expression, a "counter-language," and "anti-novel," described in *Rayuela* by Morelli.

> There are figures that I create and there are the ones that form themselves in my books. The latter are the most important.
> —*Julio Cortázar*

62: *Modelo para armar* (62: A Model Kit)

62: Modelo para armar, Julio Cortázar's third novel, appeared in print in 1968; however it was already intuited in 1963. As Cortázar explained in an author's note to the book, his intentions were "sketched out one day past in the final paragraphs of Chapter 62 of *Rayuela*, which explains the title of this book . . ." In that chapter, which forms part of *Rayuela*'s "Expendable Chapters," Morelli proposes to write a new book in which characters will interact as if compelled by some force greater than each individual alone: "foreign occupying forces, advancing in the quest of their freedom of the city; a quest superior to ourselves as individuals and one which uses us for its own ends. . . ." Now in 1973, Cortázar felt that Morelli's intent was too difficult to achieve because the characters were in danger of becoming robots.

If one has ever watched flies buzz around, motes of dust float through the air, or colored glass pieces fall in and out of place in a kaleidoscope, one can capture Cortázar's intent in *62: Modelo para armar.* The aleatory flight of flies, the Brownian movement of particles in the air, the puzzle pieces of the kaleidoscope, all create designs. Crisscrossing each other's paths, the individual insects, particles and pieces form many figures. The collective pattern becomes more meaningful and marvelous than the individual parts. In *Rayuela,* Oliveira had already sensed that he and La Maga were participants in this type of movement:

> . . .little by little, Maga, we go along forming an absurd pattern,
> . . . .
> with our movements we sketch out a pattern just like the
> . . . .
> one flies make when they fly around a room, from here to
> . . . .
> there, suddenly in mid-flight, from there to here, that's what
> . . . .
> they call Brownian movement, now do you understand?[19]

So it is also with *62: Modelo para armar* wherein the Brownian movement of characters and thoughts forms a figure more powerful than its component parts.

It is a "superior" figure according to Cortázar-Morelli since the characters seem to have little understanding and even less control over it. Morelli continues in *Rayuela*: "On the edge of social behavior, some might suspect an interaction of a different nature, a billiard game that certain individuals play or are played at, a drama with no Oedipuses, no Rastignacs, no Phaedras, an impersonal drama . . ." Herein lies one of the chief differences between *Rayuela* and *62: Modelo para armar*. In the former, Oliveira plays a game in order to save himself from reasoned reality. In the latter, it is the characters who are played with like pawns. Juan of *62: Modelo para armar* describes the characters as cards being dealt out by someone else.

62: Modelo para armar is an "impersonal" novel to the extent that its protagonist is actually a group of many characters including Juan, Hélène, Marrast, and Nicole. They are reflections and echoes of each other, crossing paths during their individual flights. It is the figure they form that is the story of *62: Modelo para armar*.

The character development—or lack of it—exposes each character's reality as a superficial fragment of a whole which is not subject to rational cause and effect analysis. The characters are deliberately sketchy, as Morelli proposed in another chapter of *Rayuela*, so that the reader will have to fill the gaps, the reasons for their actions. The emphasis, as Morelli explained, is not to be placed on the character as he reacts in a situation but rather on the situation as it reverberates in his or her mind, calling forth unexpected and illogical concatenations.

Morelli also asserts that the behavior of his characters would not be subject to current psychological interpretations:

The actors would appear to be unhealthy or complete idiots. Not that they would show themselves incapable of current *challenges and responses*: love, jealousy, pity, and so on down the line, but in them something which Homo sapiens keeps subliminal would laboriously open up a road as if a third eye were blinking out with effort from under the frontal bone.[20]

That third eye is symbolic of an unusual perspective from which the characters perceive subliminal levels of reality in close association with conscious reality. The associative flow of events and intuitions is the third eye, the new key for apprehending—although not necessarily comprehending—life.

The approach to character portrayal and novel structure is precisely this state of analogical associations in constant flux—a state characteristic of dreams, hallucinations, and nightmares. This method explains the nonchronological order of events, the free associations across time and space, the mysterious and hermetic symbols.

Interestingly enough Cortázar explained to me that *62: Modelo para armar* was born of a recurring dream that he has had since he was a young man. In that dream he goes into the city, as it is described in *62* and feels compelled to seek out someone or something in a hotel. Often the dream attains nightmare proportions. First, he wrote the poem which appears in the novel, and he thought that it would serve as an exorcism, freeing him from the nightmare thereafter. A few weeks later it returned. While he was writing the novel, the dream disappeared but it has come back again. "It's sort of a Hell, a Hell seen as a strange city."

Cortázar's novel is a vertiginous juxtaposition of

the characters' experiences in two different, although not completely separate, realms: the zone and the City. The zone is the meeting place of the "in group," much like the gatherings of the Serpent Club in *Rayuela*. In *62: Modelo para armar* the zone exists during the time in which the characters meet to play games and to share unusual experiences. In this way, they temporarily escape from mundane life, its emptiness and futility.

The City has an antecedent in the mysterious Paris of the short story "The Other Heaven." At first the City appears written with a capital letter. Although both the City in the novel and the Paris of the short story are recognizable by their arcades and a similar atmosphere of mystery and horror, in *62: Modelo para armar* the City is a more oneiric region into which some of the characters wander. Unlike the Paris of "The Other Heaven," the City has no geographic limitations, even though it is characterized by high sidewalks, a hotel with labyrinthine rooms and streetcars.

In the zone, the characters attempt to be masters of their own destiny, to control their circumstances in order to negate mundane life. In the City the characters are obsessively compelled to participate in searches over which they have little control and even less understanding. The zone of the conscious individual in his circumstance and the City of the subconscious experience join to flirt dangerously with each other in *62: Modelo para armar*. The interaction creates a state of dream wakefulness.

Let us then sketch the main characters, the pieces in this model kit. Juan is an Argentinean interpreter living in Paris. He loves Hélène although she does not reciprocate those feelings. Juan travels a great deal accompanied by his lover, a sensual Danish woman named Tell. He uses her sexuality as an evasion and repose from Paris. Much of the novel focuses on Juan's thoughts and actions, his wanderings in the City where he pursues Hélène, and above all, the associations he captures between events and people.

Hélène is an anesthetist whose cold, hostile, and distant exterior protects her from solitude by means of a well-ordered existence. Celia, a young student at the Sorbonne, describes her as sad and dead. When Celia runs away from her family, she is invited home by Hélène. The anesthetist mysteriously attracts the other characters who seem to dance "around her, around the Hélène light, a kind of Hélène reason . . ." Despite her well-ordered exterior, Hélène is obsessed with the death of a young man in the hospital where she works. She associates him with Juan since he looked very much like him. A lesbian, Hélène is as much at home sexually with Celia—whom she seduces—as with Juan with whom she also makes love. In the City she carries a heavy package whose string cuts her fingers. There she is compelled to keep a mysterious appointment in the hotel of labyrinthine rooms.

Nicole and Marrast form another part of the figure. They reside in Paris and visit London where Marrast is looking for an oilclotch stone. He is an artist commissioned by the town of Arcueil to sculpt a statue of the hero Vercingetorix. Like a good cronopio he creates the statue and pedestal in an inverted order. Marrast is bored with life. His antics seem to be an effort to fill the emptiness of existence.

One day he sees an advertisement in the news: "Are you sensitive, intelligent, anxious or a little lonely?

Neurotics Anonymous are a lively, mixed group who believe that the individual is unique. Details s.a.e., Box 8662." He writes a letter in answer to the advertisement suggesting that the neurotics would be more useful to society if they would gather in the second gallery of the Courtauld Institute to resolve the enigma of a painting by Tilly Kettle—a portrait of Dr. Daniel Lysons, D.C.L., M.D. holding a branch of *Hermodactylus tuberosis.* The anonymous letter causes unusual crowds of neurotics to appear in gallery two, necessitates extra guards, and finally upsets the director so much that he removes the painting.

During his gallery visits, Marrast becomes acquainted with one of the neurotics, the young lutist Austin, whom he later tutors in French. Although Marrast feels it is useless to confront life in a serious, logical manner, and thus his unusual adventures, he also senses that life is a hopeless void: "doubt, a hollow, hope, a hollow, even larger, rancor, the hollow of hollows, modalities of the great hole, of what I had fought against all my life with hammer and chisel, a few women, and tons of wasted clay." His frustrations, in part, are due to his love for Nicole.

Nicole illustrates childrens books with pictures of gnomes. Although she no longer loves Marrast she continues to live with him. During a trip from Venice to Mantua, as they pass by some red houses, Nicole tells Marrast of her love for Juan. Later in London Nicole wishes that Marrast would seek a sadistic revenge: ". . . how I wait for the punishment that I'm incapable of inflicting on myself." Marrast dreams about her and names her the malcontent, the girl held prisoner. Nicole finally seduces Austin in order to force Marrast to break with her. On the way back to Paris from the unveiling of Marrast's statue in Arcueil she gets off the train, enters the City and walks suicidally toward the canal. Near the end of the novel Juan sees her on a barge, about to jump into the water.

Austin, the lutist and former neurotic, is innocent in matters of love. He has humorous sexual adventures with a whore, Georgette, who insists that he not ruin her coiffure. During his French lessons with Marrast, Austin expressed his socialist ideas to the group. He considers their antics in the Courtauld Institute to be senseless in view of a greater necessity for socio-political reform. His character is a precursor of the theme in *Libro de Manuel*, Cortázar's latest novel. When Celia travels to London, fleeing from Hélène, Austin and she become lovers. He boasts to Celia of his sexual prowess, his ability to make her live as a woman for the first time. She then confesses her involuntary lesbian experience with Hélène. Near the end of the story, Austin enters the City to wait for Hélène in the hotel room. There he kills her in revenge.

These characters who form a nuclear group in the novel are joined by two Argentines, Calac and Polanco —referred to as the Tartars or the pampa savages—and by their "paredros." Calac and Polanco are cronopios who attach a lawn mower motor to a rowboat and find themselves propelled onto an island in the middle of a pond that has tides, rising of course. They carry on senseless conversations in the subway provoking curiosity in the crowds; and they often speak using neologisms.

The "paredros" is an interesting and elusive character: "a kind of buddy or substitute or babysitter for the exceptional." The "paredros," as explained by Cortázar, is an Egyptian term which describes a type of double of an Egyptian deity, an associated god which can complement or replace or assist the divinity under certain circumstances. Cortázar uses the term in an extra-religious sense in *62: Modelo para armar*; however, he had already employed a similar interpretation of "doubles" in his short stories and in *Rayuela.* In the latter, Oliveira describes the alter ego; this image will give birth to the "paredros" in *62: Modelo para armar*:

> It's very simple, every exaltation or depression pushes me towards a state suitable for
> I will call them paravisions
> That is to say (that's the worst of it, saying it)
> an instantaneous aptitude for going out, so that suddenly I can grasp myself from outside, or from inside but on a different plane,
> as if I were somebody who was looking at me
> (better still—because in reality I cannot see myself—: like someone who is living me).[21]

Any one character can be another's paredros. At times, however, the paredros emerges by himself, looking at the characters from outside. He is a "paravision" that takes shape in the zone and participates in conversations and events.

Cortázar points out in the author's note to the novel that the intent of the subtitle *A Model Kit* does not relate to the structure of paragraphs or to the writing as much as to the level of meaning in the novel "where the opening for combinatory art is more insistent and imperative." The novel's meaning is, as Marrast asserts, "like putting together the pieces of an erector set without thinking about any particular structure, and suddenly . . ." Cortázar begins to expose the pieces of the model kit to us when Juan sits down in the Polidor restaurant. Facing a wall of mirrors, he overhears a diner ask for a "château saignant." That phrase initiates a network of associations in his mind which he and we slowly decipher as the novel progresses.

"Château saignant" is a shortened form of "châteaubriand saignant," which is a kind of "rare steak" in French. These words call forth to Juan a series of coincidental events in his life. That day before entering the Polidor, he had bought a book by Michel Butor. In it he finds a description of Niagara Falls by the author of *René* and *Atala*, the Frenchman Châteaubriand. If the reader is familiar with the book to which Juan refers, *Niagara (6810000 litres d'eau par seconde; étude stéréphonique*) published in 1965 in France, he will discern a clever association between Butor, a French "new novelist," and Julio Cortázar.[22] Butor's *Niagara* is a collage of events and observations across time and space revolving around the hub of Niagara Falls much as Cortázar has Juan's associations revolve around the phrase "château saignant." In fact, like Cortázar in the "Table of Instructions" to *Rayuela* and in an author's note to *62: Modelo para armar*, Butor in an author's note to *Niagara* invites the reader to combine the collage pieces at will: "Since the mobility of reading is much greater than that of any listening, you may imagine, with book in hand, all kinds of combinations."[23] When asked if he had intentionally referred to Butor's book because of this coincidence, Cortázar admitted that he really knew very little about that author and his books, even though the reference in *62: Modelo para armar* did allude to *Niagara*. This, then, would seem to be one of the figures "unconsciously" and mysteriously formed by itself in Cortázar's novels.

"Château saignant" also recalls another related word, "sanglant," which means bloody; therefore, the phrase "château saignant" on a different level of interpretation signifies "bloody castle." From this nucleus Juan's chain of associations is born again.

A "bloody castle" calls forth two related images, the countess and Frau Marta. From the Polidor restaurant Juan senses a connection between Transylvania, the birthplace of vampire tales, and Sylvaner, the beverage he orders:

> . . . and to order without previous reflection a bottle of Sylvaner, which contained in its first syllables, as in a charade, the middle syllables of the word in which there beat in turn the geographic center of an obscure ancestral terror, couldn't really go beyond a mediocre phonetic association.[24]

In "Lejana," with Alina Reyes the reader has already seen the magically disturbing world that opens from a mere word association.

In Vienna on a business trip, accompanied by Tell, Juan visits the Basilisken Haus (House of the Basilisk) on the Blutgasse (Blood Street). The building exudes the mystery of vampire tales. Legends tell of the Blood Countess, Erzebet Bathori, who lived there at times. She bled and tortured girls in her castle and bathed in their blood. The Gothic horror of those tales invades Tell and Juan who associate the vampirism of centuries ago with the intentions of Frau Marta, another guest at the same hotel. She has befriended a young English girl. One night Juan and Tell follow Frau Marta through the halls of the hotel. They discover her entering the English girl's room. There she undresses the girl who hypnotically and passively stares at the lantern light. Juan and Tell's presence, however, seems to thwart Frau Marta's desire of vampirism or lesbianism, much as the appearance of Michel prevented the homosexual encounter in the short story "Las babas del diablo." As Tell and Juan watch, Frau Marta and the girl leave the room and become lost in the City.

Near the end of the story when Hélène confesses her affair with Celia, Juan realizes why he seemed to link the countess, Frau Marta, and Hélène as he sat in the Polidor restaurant. All three women attacked young girls: the countess bound them for bloodletting, Frau Marta pursued the English girl, and Hélène seduced Celia. Juan had been suppressing thoughts of Hélène's lesbianism by replacing her with Frau Marta in his mind:

"In the Blutgasse," Juan thought. Closing his eyes, he rejected the recurrent image, the light from the dark lantern on the floor, the corner from where he would have to keep on walking in search of Hélène. But Celia, then—what had she looked for in Celia? Even though he fought with all his strength, he felt the fingers of the image closing over Hélène, and he had always known it, even since that Christmas eve, the corner of the Rue de Vaugirard, opposite that mirror with wreaths, I caught up with you in some way. I knew what I refuse to accept now. I was afraid and appealed to anything so as not to believe. I loved you too much to accept that hallucination where you weren't even present, where you were only a mirror or a book or a shadow in a castle. I lost myself in analogies and bottles of white wine. I got to the brink and preferred not to know. I consented to not knowing, even though I could have, Hélène. Everything was telling me that, and now I realize that I could have known the truth, have accepted the fact that you were . . .[25]

The third associative configuration is somewhat more complex and eventually converges with the previous correspondences. It has a dual base in the symbol of the basilisk and the object of the doll. The basilisk is a fabulous animal with a snake's body and a three pointed crest. In medieval times it was said to be born of an egg laid by a cock and hatched by a toad. Its glance was thought to be lethal so that it could be destroyed only by looking at itself in a mirror. In *62: Modelo para armar* the symbol of the basilisk appears several times. Juan visits the Basilisken Haus in Vienna; the royal crest of the Bathoris contains a dragon biting its tail; Hélène wears a brooch in the shape of a basilisk or a lizard; and Monsieur Ochs owns a ring with a basilisk on it.

Monsieur Ochs is also a link between the basilisk and the doll. He lives in Paris and enjoys manufacturing perverse dolls which contain money inside of them or obscene objects—like a polychrome phallus. Little girls discover the contents if their dolls break open; or mothers who have heard of the money disembowel the dolls to find it. One day Monsieur Ochs gives Juan a gift of a doll. Since Juan knows of Monsieur Ochs's strange products and has informed Tell of them, he playfully gives the doll to Tell in Vienna. She in turn, without suspecting the contents, decides to send it to Hélène. In Hélène's apartment, Celia puts it to bed, much as Hélène had taken care of the young man who died in the hospital. The morning after their lesbian encounter, Celia throws the doll to the floor. It lies there as if it were a dead baby, cut open with "something sticking out through the crack."

Using the basilisk, the doll, and vampirism as keys, many coincidences fall into place to form a figure. The countess Erzebet Bathori, evoked by the Basilisken Haus, pricked the necks of her victims to draw blood; Frau Marta in Vienna also violated the English girl; and Hélène describes her violation of Celia in Paris in terms of a "needle sticking into an arm." Of course, she is also describing how she administered the anesthesia to the young man who later died. She cared for him in the hospital but he died opened up on the operating table "the way dolls are opened to see what they have inside"; the way Monsieur Ochs's dolls are disembowled by mothers; the way Hélène's doll was smashed by Celia. All of these events violate a victim in some way.

The reverberating chain of events congeals even more. Hélène's heavy package now fuses with the doll —symbolic of her guilt in the death of the young man. She carries one within the other along with her in the City. Since she compares Juan with the dead man, she feels that Juan will be waiting for her in the City to absolve her of her guilt by receiving the package. Ironically, however, it is Austin who waits to kill her in revenge for her violation of his lover Celia.

62: Modelo para armar is a disconcerting novel for it tells of desire without love. Despite the few humorous interludes, the initial hermeticism of the symbols, and the pseudo-vampirism, the novel's main theme emerges as a story of ill-fated relationships among the characters. Desire is always tinged with egoism, sadism, lesbianism, idealism or indifference, but rarely with unselfish and sharing love.

Juan uses Tell as an object of desire in order to escape routine: "I put you there and I take you away, I cork you and I uncork you, I take you with me to drop you when it's time to be sad or to be alone. And you, on the other hand, never made an object out of me . . ." Tell recognizes her strange mother-lover role full well for she calls herself the great consoler: "I invent night for him, not only in the predictable sense . . . but I wash words off him, wash off earning a living, not having the courage to resign from what he doesn't like, that it's me and not Hélène that he undresses slowly in his bitter fever." She realizes that everything he gives her is really meant for Hélène and even assures him that if she can she will bring Hélène to him. Tell, however, conserves her freedom only because she withholds some of her love: "How lucky that I don't love you too much, my handsome! How lucky that I'm free, that I give you my time and everything you like without its bothering me too much. . . ."

Juan's love for Hélène is an idealistic impossibility. Whereas he accepts Tell as a sensual woman, he cannot conceive of Hélène as a woman with sexual aberrations, she must be idealistically perfect. Even when Hélène gives herself to Juan, she promises nothing. She fears that unintentionally she has harmed him—the young man in the hospital—and will continue to do so. She assures him, however, that she is incapable of sadism and also that she is incapable of love in terms of custom and routine. When she discloses her affair with Celia, Juan leaves. As if the Hélène he had just made love to in the zone could not possibly fit the concept of

Hélène he had sought in the City, he enters the City once again in search of his ideal.

Cortázar explained his identification with Juan, saying that he would have liked him to have more luck than he does in the book. He also noted that the character of Hélène was based on a woman he had seen briefly and met superficially. "I don't know Hélène very well. I would have liked to know her better."

Marrast and Nicole's relationship is also ill-fated and masochistic. When she uses Austin to break with the passive routine of her relationship with Marrast—which she feels is harming him even more than her—he calls her a whore. Not even Austin and Celia in their new love for one another seem to be free of desire without love. Even in that relationship Austin displays egoism for he feels that Celia did not exist until he made love to her. In *62: Modelo para armar*, love is sex, desire, guilt, or idealism but hardly ever a shared and mutually giving relationship either sexually or intellectually.

Cortázar continues to experiment with language in this third novel as he did in *Rayuela*: neologisms, invented conversations, word games, elliptical dialogue, and shifts in narrative perspective. However there are notable differences. *Rayuela*'s language is often cerebral and concentrated; whereas *62: Modelo para armar* is poetic and diffuse. The former appeals with its text, the latter with its tone and texture. Nevertheless the same feeling that language betrays man pervades both novels. Marrast calls words "stuffing."

62: Modelo para armar is not an optimistic novel, as was *Rayuela*. Oliveira may or may not leap onto the hopscotch at the end of the novel: possibilities allow for hope. At the end of *62: Modelo para armar*, Hélène is dead, Nicole equally as fated, and only Feuille Morte —her name means "dead leaf" in French—is met at the train station in Paris. She is the only character in the novel who never speaks an intelligible word. Although a minor character, her playful, childlike conduct endears her to the others who protect her and watch over her. The novel ends with the paredros standing by a lamppost watching the insects move aimlessly about and with the appearance of Feuille Morte: " 'Bisbis bisbis,' said Feuille Morte."

After having submitted to the chain of associations in *62: Modelo para armar*, one cannot refrain from attempting a symbolic interpretation of this last scene by comparing it to a passage in *Rayuela*, where Oliveira talks of dead leaves and lamps, the same two elements of the final scene in *62:*

> I bring the dry leaves back to my flat and paste them on a lampshade. . . . I keep on thinking about all the leaves I will not see, the gatherer of dry leaves, about so many things that there must be in the air and which these eyes will not see, poor bats out of novels and movies and dried flowers. There must be lamps everywhere, there must be leaves that I will never see.[26]

Certainly Juan and Cortázar himself have tried to capture all the invisible figures that float in the air including the "dead leaf" in the pages of *62: Modelo para armar*.

Cortázar has noted that *62* was the hardest of his novels to write because the rules imposed on him by the structure were very strict and he respected them. "When I finished it, I was more than content, I was relieved."

Yes, it's always one of the female
characters who crosses over or shows
the man the way.
—*Julio Cortázar*

Libro de Manuel (Book of Manuel)

Libro de Manuel is Cortázar's novel of social commitment. He wrote it in order to expose the systematic torture of political prisoners in many Latin American countries and in so doing to help stop such violence. Since most of his other books were best sellers all over Latin America, Cortázar knew that *Libro de Manuel* would have a wide circulation and hopefully be a significant influence. In March 1973 during a visit to Buenos Aires to commemorate the release of this novel, Cortázar contributed his authorship rights to two Argentinean organizations that aid the families of political prisoners.

Libro de Manuel clearly reflects the author's political "coming of age." After many visits to Cuba and to Chile, Cortázar has concluded that the only road for Latin America is the socialist way. And yet this fourth novel is not a political treatise. This is due in part to the fact that the distribution of such a treatise might have been censored or that its audience might have been limited. But it is also due to the fact that Cortázar, like the novel's protagonist Andrés, finds himself personally between two worlds—middle-class comfort and socialist commitment—neither of which he is able to deny or embrace fully. A blind, unilaterally pure socialism and a fanatical adherence to inflexible principles frighten him. Neither can he totally escape his bourgeois origins. Above all he refuses to deny his individual freedom to express his vitality by every means possible regardless of whether or not that expression adheres to a strict party line. Cortázar, like Andrés, is aware of the shortcomings of any pure ideology, and yet, he chooses to join the revolution as the best hope for Latin American reality.

In this novel Julio Cortázar has chosen to forge his revolution by means of a bizarre mixture of fantasy and fact: the plot is imaginary but the news articles inserted in the text are factual. In the opening pages he claims that this combination will surely please neither fiction lovers nor history fans. His introduction states:

> What counts, what I've tried to tell, is the affirmative sign as opposed to the gamut of scorn and horror, and that affirmation has to be the most solar, the most vital part of man: his erotic and ludic thirst, his liberation from taboos, his claim to a shared dignity on an earth freed at last from this daily horizon of fangs and dollars.[27]

Libro de Manuel relates the kidnapping of a Latin American diplomat by a group of unusual guerrillas in Paris. The story is told from the double and, at times, confused perspective of two characters: Andrés, who is indecisive about joining the group, and a member of the group who is jokingly referred to as "you know who." The latter observer takes notes on the assault plans and execution, the former reads the notes and thus uncovers the plot of the novel.

The action is interrupted periodically to allow for the insertion of articles from French and Latin American newspapers read by the group members. The clippings appear in the original although reduced print for, as Cortázar explained, he wanted to assure the reader of their authenticity. The articles announce individual protests against societal pressures which usurp personal liberties and exact conformity; they tell of the consistent torture of political prisoners in countries such as Brazil, Uruguay, and Argentina; they relate guerrilla activities in Latin America and Europe; they expose societal taboos, such as those concerning homosexuality; and they exhibit the linguistic peculiarities of the Spanish language in different countries. The kidnappers gather the articles for Susanna and Patricio, two members of the group who are assembling a scrapbook for their baby boy, Manuel. This book of Manuel is destined to educate the child as well as the reader to actual instances of protest, change and revolution in Latin American societies.

The characters in *Libro de Manuel* are as internationally representative as were those of *Rayuela* or *62: Modelo para armar* and include Argentineans, Frenchmen, a Pole, a Panamanian and a Chilean. They participate in sorties into middle-class complacent society in order to incite unrest. Their adventures consist of Robin Hood robberies of dispensaries and the subsequent distribution of the booty to the poor people; of sudden screams in dark movie houses; of loud comments in large crowds about outrageous prices in food stores or unsanitary conditions in department stores; and of eating while standing up at a table in a fashionable restaurant.

Although the group's mini-provocations mature into a large scale kidnapping, referred to as the "Joda," this serious and dangerous plan in no way denies the playful atmosphere of the group's other undertakings. Quite in keeping with Cortázar's reverence for game, humor, and imagination, the "Joda" becomes the nucleus for a strange mixture of guerrilla activity and fraternity-type pranks. The unusual plan is also described with a language that uses humorous words and neologisms such as the "Joda"*—defined by Cortázar as "screwing around" or "fooling around"—and various forms of words developed from the base "hormigas," ants, to describe the Latin American henchmen who are used as much to protect the diplomat as to attempt to assassinate him in order to later blame the guerrillas.

The plans unfold in the following manner. Old man Collins produced $20,000 of counterfeit money which is smuggled into France by two Argentineans—Gladis the airline stewardess and Oscar, who poses as a representative of a Latin American zoological society. The money is hidden in the false linings of two thermal containers which house three fantastically imaginary animals, a turquoise penguin and two "peludos reales," gifts to the zoo at Vincennes. With falsified documents, the guerrillas, pretending to be representative of the Vincennes Zoo, ceremoniously meet Oscar at the airport for the transferral of the containers. Later the bills extracted from the linings, are cashed simultaneously at

* Although in Argentina the usual word for "to copulate" is "coger," another Spanish word more commonly used in Spain is "joder" from which "joda" derives. Cortázar explained that for Argentineans "joder" is not used in a sexual sense; however, it also has the following connotations: "to bother someone" and "to make fun of someone." Cortázar added, "From those two meanings my 'Joda' was born because they are expressed in the kidnapping."

many banks in Paris. Shortly afterwards the diplomat is kidnapped and held in exchange for the release of Latin American political prisoners. The group, however, is apprehended by the French police and so the "Joda" ends with the deportation of many of the members and with Andrés compiling "you know who's" notes which tell of the entire adventure.

Cortázar reveals particular preference for certain characters, especially for those who deviate from a purely political approach to the Joda. Andrés, the protagonist, is one of those, for he reflects the most doubt concerning the activities of the group engaged in these acts of societal provocation in Paris. When he compares these attacks on Parisian bourgeois society to guerrilla kidnappings and activities in Latin America announced in the press, he considers the former to be mere useless tokenism.

His dilemma is worsened, however, for he has a dream which obsesses him, a dream which Cortázar himself experienced after he began to write the novel. Andrés dreams that he is watching a movie by Fritz Lang when the usher escorts him behind stage to meet a Cuban who awaits him. Although he remembers that in the dream he enters the room, meets the man, and then leaves, he cannot recall the actual scene with the Cuban or the message that the stranger gave him to carry out. The elusive significance of the dream haunts him. When he finally joins the kidnap group the dream's meaning is symbolically revealed as a call for commitment to revolution. The Cuban's message is "Wake up!"

However, Andrés's indecision about joining the group, is but one of his predicaments as a man who straddles two generations seeking a bridge between the old society and the new revolution. Andrés, like many of Cortázar's other characters, Oliveira, for instance, also finds himself between two women, the Polish actress Ludmilla, with whom he lives, and the French woman Francine. The triangle becomes more complicated than he had expected when Lud, attracted to the group's activities and to one of its leaders, Marcos, leaves Andrés. She serves as a catalyst to Andrés's decision to join the Joda, for it is not only revolutionary commitment but also a need to see Lud again that forces him to seek out the guerrilla hiding place. In fact, at times Andrés's erotic preoccupation seems to usurp the political focus of *Libro de Manuel.*

The social commitment is altered, as well, and intentionally so, by means of two other characters favored by Cortázar in the novel: Lonstein and Oscar. They both also approach the Joda and revolution in an unusual way. Lonstein is as absolutely Argentinean as he is Jewish. A declared masturbator, he washes dead bodies in the morgue, cultivates a strange toadstool from which there emanates a green phosphorescence and speaks in an imaginative language whose musical rhythm and sonority is one of the novel's principle attributes. It is a mixture of an Argentinean slang called "lunfardo," of pure invention, and of neologisms based on French—"femucha" from "femme" meaning woman—and on phonetic English such as "friyider," "andicapeados," and "kidnapeados." As Cortázar explained, it is not necessary to understand each of Lonstein's words in order to capture the meaning of the passage. Cortázar holds a particular affection for Lonstein because of his defiance of social taboos and his imaginative expression.

Oscar also differs considerably from the pure revolutionary stereotype. He is obsessed by news of an escape attempt made by inmates of a women's reformatory in Argentina and by Monique's story of the rebellion of a group of girls at a religious school in France. Fragmentary scenes of both uprisings against societal authority flash through his mind mingling with the reality of the Joda. In this way Cortázar, emotionally rather than intellectually, links revolt on many levels by briefly associating key words and passages.

Libro de Manuel is the defiant assertion of an author who embraces socialist revolution but also warns that he will not sacrifice his personal freedom—his erotic rites, his aesthetic preferences, his imagination and his humor—for any ideology. In the closing pages of *Libro de Manuel* the following dialogue between Andrés and Patricio, one of the more pure revolutionaries, demonstrates that assertion:

> . . . And now I'm leaving because it's late; I have to look for a record by Joni Mitchell that they promised me and keep on arranging what "you know who" left us.
>
> In that order of preference?—Patricio said looking him in the eye.—Your Joni what's-her-name and afterwards the other?
>
> I don't know—said Andrés—it'll be that way or the opposite but it'll always be both.[28]

Near the end of the novel, fiction and fantasy yield to fact. Twelve of the last fifteen pages are devoted to excerpts from two sources: the testimony of political prisoners before a human rights press conference denouncing actual cases of torture of political prisoners in Argentina, and an extract from *Conversations with North Americans* of testimony taken by the lawyer Mark Lane from thirty-two Vietnam veterans. The latter attest to instances of torture for which the veterans were trained and commended during that war.

The columns of atrocities run on unbearably in parallel columns until finally Cortázar breaks off his shock treatment, that is really the purpose of the novel, with a statistical table from the United States Department of Defense printed in 1969. It shows the numbers of Latin American Military Personnel by country trained in the United States. The inference is obviously that the United States aids oppressive Latin American regimes in their torture tactics by training their police. In our interview Cortázar maintained that he was also as strongly indicting Latin Americans for brutality against their own brothers.

On the very last page, true to the open-end approach to all of his novels, Cortázar returns to fiction and leaves the reader the choice of interpreting a mysterious scene. Once again, as with his other three novels, death is present. In the morgue Lonstein is washing a corpse as light filters onto the dead man's face. Lonstein muses about how no one will believe this story, "they'll think we invented it all." Is the corpse Marcos who was perhaps killed in the kidnapping fray, or "you know who" who mysteriously disappeared at the end of the novel, or a torture victim, ever-present across time and space as a result of the news and testimony included in the novel or perhaps the symbol of Andrés's dead bourgeois lack of commitment? Cortázar has said that it pleased him greatly to hear so many possibilities and that he himself did not know exactly who the dead man was. Nevertheless, after having written the novel, he had the following thoughts:

When I reread the part about the corpse in the morgue, there are two references that made me think of something I hadn't thought of before when I was writing, something I see you haven't thought of either, that is the photograph of the dead Che Guevara that was distributed all over the world. The head, they say, just as I had written, was slightly raised and the eyes were not completely closed. And there's a flicker of light that filters through the lids and Lonstein tells him, "look at me all you want, it's all right." There's something in the description of that corpse that is also Che. So I add another possibility to the choices. But it wasn't intentional because that would have been "cheap."

3

The Book As Sponge

If I had the technical means to print my own books,
I think I would keep on producing collage-books.
—Julio Cortázar

Julio Cortázar has written four books and many articles which do not conform to either the novel or short story genre. Most recently he has published a collection of poetry entitled *Pameos y meopas*, 1971 (Pameos and Meopas) and a lyrical book entitled *Prosa del observatorio*, 1972 (Prose from the Observatory). The latter is a reflection on the "figures" formed by the stars and the life cycle of eels. It was inspired by a newspaper article in 1971 in *Le Monde* and a visit to the observatories of the Sultan Jai Singh in India in 1968. Cortázar's photographs of the observatories illustrate the volume.

His most outstanding contributions, however, to a "potpourri" genre are *La vuelta al día en ochenta mundos* (1967) and *Ultimo Round* (1969). These two books are biographical collages for the author reveals himself and his preferences through anecdotes, reflections, essays, and poems about everything that fascinates or amuses him. Amidst a melange of photographs, drawings and engravings, the reader is entertained by a diverse and original offering of the important and the trivial. The entire gamut of the reader's taste can fairly prickle at flavors ranging from white humor to black humor, nonsense to intellectualism, sarcasm, wit, lyricism and social commentary.

La vuelta al día en ochenta mundos is a joy to read, even to browse. It's title of course, was born of Julio Cortázar's affection for his namesake Jules Verne whose books were his favorites as a young boy. In *La vuelta al día en ochenta mundos*, which contains many engravings of scenes and characters from Verne's works, the Argentinean Julio exposes us to the treasures of at least eighty of his worlds in one book.

Another namesake participates in this fine volume, the Argentine artist Julio Silva, whose drawings of fantastic creatures populate the pages as well as the cover, on which two boys engaged in leap frog slowly metamorphose into frogs. In Cortázar's summer home in Saignon, France, hangs a large painting by Julio Silva, a dynamic and haunting group of creatures playfully and yet mischievously joining claw, beak and hand in a dance across the living room wall. Cortázar and Silva are presently planning to collaborate on another book.

The engraving on the title page significantly depicts an aquarium in which all sorts of strange animals in metamorphosis swim: a bird-fish, a horse-fish, a dog-fish, a cow-fish, a cat-fish. Anything is possible in this unique volume, full of surprises. Cortázar characterizes it as sponge-like:

> All that follows takes part as much as possible . . . in that respiration of a sponge in which fish-like memories are continually going in and out; like explosive connections of time and space and matter that sobriety, that lady we listen to too much, would consider irreconcilable.[1]

The brief selections basically deal with memories, personal daily experiences, literature, and politics. Quotes are extravagantly employed, for as Cortázar assures us, "To quote someone is to quote oneself." In various selections the author recalls his summer home and the beautiful valleys near Saignon, he remembers his famous compatriot Jorge Luis Borges in a poem; he reminisces about his own travels as an interpreter; and then he criticizes nostalgic memories for their false idealism.

The literary selections include critical comments on the lack of humor and naturalness in Argentinean writing and his praise for writers such as the Cuban Lezama Lima. He also offers some of his own short stories and poems. Cortázar manifests his affection for certain surrealist writers and painters—Roussel, Desnos, Duchamp, Artaud, Ernst, Dalí, Delvaux, Man Ray—as well as for other authors and actors as diverse as Keats, Shakespeare and Buster Keaton.

The author dedicates many selections to fellow cronopios. He writes about jazz greats like Louis Armstrong, Thelonious Monk and Clifford Brown and illustrates the pages with photographs of them. Boxers are one of his favorite subjects as well. Insanity and genius attract his attention in anecdotes about an insane painter named Wölfli and the strange inventor Juan Esteban Fassio, two others that Cortázar would call cronopios.

Cortázar's fascination for mystery and murderers is apparent in the selection entitled "Relaciones sospechosas" (Suspicious Relations). There he discusses his theory of victimology: the murder victim's perverse attraction to his killer. He cites the case histories of Jack the Ripper and Peter Kürten, the vampire of Düsseldorf. During our interview, as we sat outside his summer home at nightfall, Cortázar explained this interest in murderers and their victims. He confessed to being an amateur criminologist and vampirologist. As a small bat suddenly darted from the eaves of his house, he laughed and quickly assured me that it was not of the vampire species.

Cortázar also reveals his obsessions in at least two selections: "Estación de la mano" (The Time of the Hand) and "La caricia más profunda" (The Most Profound Caress). The former, an early romantic story which he thought he had burned, he published in his first miscellany for nostalgic reasons. It is about a hand named Dg which comes to visit him until one day the author becomes suspicious of it. Sensing his mistrust, the hand never returns. Cortázar has remained fascinated with hands in his other works like "No One's to Blame," and he confesses that he sometimes dreams of hands and gloves capable of independent life. He cannot sleep if a glove is out of a drawer unless he places a book on top of it. He fears that a hand will come to fill it. Likewise, he explained, his obsessive fear of being buried alive finds expression in "The Most Profound Caress." There a man walking about the city finds himself slowly sinking into the earth. When he arrives at his fiancée's house he is staring directly at her shoes.

A few of Cortázar's principal themes such as "figures" are related to his life in anecdotes like "De otra máquina célibe" (About Another Celibate Machine). Some of his ideas about the fantastic short stories that he writes and the genesis of at least one, "Torito," are discussed in "Del sentimiento de lo fantástico" (About the Sentiment of Fantasy) and "El noble arte" (The Noble Art.) One might borrow and alter the title of a short selection in *La vuelta al día en ochenta mundos* to subtitle this kaleidoscopic endeavor not as "Viaje a un país de cronopios" (A Trip to The

Land of Cronopios) but as "A Trip to The Land of Julio the Cronopio."

Ultimo Round continues the tradition of a biographically revealing medley of miscellaneous writings. Once again Julio Silva collaborated in this book and suggested the unusual format which consists of a volume cut into two sections of uneven dimensions. The sections labeled "ground floor" and "first floor" can be read separately. The books covers are designed with quotes and columns of articles enticing the browser to seek out certain selections within: "*Bicycles*: There are more things on a bicycle than what your philosophy imagines, Horace. Information on p. 70, ground floor."

Ultimo Round differs from Cortázar's first volume of miscellaneous work in that it concedes more space to politics, the revolution, and eroticism. It contains some of Cortázar's best erotic poetry which is almost entirely lacking in his volume of poetry *Pameos y Meopas*. The same free reign of imagination pervades the photographs, many taken by Cortázar himself, and anecdotes such as "El Tesoro de la Juventud" (The Treasure of Youth). This selection describes the progress man had made in transportation from jets to propeller planes to ships to trains to bicycles to swimming; and, before you know it, Cortázar explains, he'll be capable of walking.

The cronopios, the memories, the literary and artistic preferences, the humor, the art, the imagination are all in *Ultimo Round*, as well as the structural and stylistic playfulness of the "man-child" Julio Cortázar in "Ya no quedan esperanza de" (There's no hope left now). In this anecdote, as previously in "La hoguera donde arde una" (The Fire Where One Burns) of *La vuelta al día en ochenta mundos* and more recently in *Libro de Manuel*, the author ingeniously tells a story employing incomplete sentences. He explained this technique to me, noting that very often in conversations people do not finish their sentences and yet one can understand the meaning quite well. He decided to employ this phenomenon as a technique in his writing.

Amid pataphysics, erotic photographs of dolls, mutable poetry and memories of Saignon, Julio Cortázar winks at us through the pages of *Ultimo Round* as if assuring the reader in his own contradictory manner, that this book is far from being *his* last round.

4

The Accomplice-Writer

I'm never interested in where I'm going
I just want to go.
—*Julio Cortázar*

When asked to comment on the omnipresence of death in his fiction, especially at the end of his four novels, Cortázar offered the following explanation:

> Precisely because at heart I am someone who is very optimistic and very vital, that is, someone who believes profoundly in life and who lives as intensely as possible, the option of death is also very strong for me. I have no religious leanings. And so the notion of death for me is one which I cannot hide or cover up or even seek consolation for in the idea of a resurrection or a second life. For me death is a scandal. It is a great scandal. It is the true scandal. I think we shouldn't have to die and that the only advantage that animals have over us is that they are ignorant of death. An animal doesn't know he's going to die. Man knows. He knows and he reacts in different ways, historically or personally. I just finished telling you my reaction and it's because of that that you have to understand that death is an extremely important and ever-present element in everything that I have written.

Cortázar exudes literary and personal vitality. He himself senses it: "I believe that I was much less vital as a young man than today." Often critics have commented on Cortázar's boyish appearance. When we discussed his facility for depicting boys and adolescents, Cortázar offered this statement which demonstrates a youthful attitude, as well: "I am still very much a boy and am adolescent in many ways. In my life relationships, in my feelings, there is an adolescent element that prevails in me. In that sense I think I am never going to get old. No, I don't change, I don't feel myself changing."

Julio Cortázar is presently planning to publish another collection of fantastic stories, five of which are already written. "But you know that I don't write the short stories. They write themselves. So they have to come to me. At the moment none are coming. But I'm beckoning them a little because I feel like writing three more and publishing them." He assured me that they would not be ideologically oriented at all, as was *Libro de Manuel.* I reminded him that many of his socialist readers in Latin America would decry such uncommitted literature, as they had done in the past. Like a boxer once again stepping into the ring he smiled and jokingly quipped, "Of course, they're going to come at me with both fists."*

* On February 17, 1974, Cortázar wrote to say that his new book of eight short stories would be released before the summer of 1974 by Alianza in Madrid perhaps in collaboration with Sudamericana in Buenos Aires. It is entitled *Octaedro.*

Notes

A Swiss Cheese Reality

1. Cortázar, "Algunos aspectos del cuento," *Casa de las Américas*, Habana, 11, 15–16, Nov. 1962–Feb. 1963, pp. 3–14.
2. Luis Harss and Barbara Dohmann, *Into the Mainstream*, New York, Harper and Row, 1966, p. 221.
3. Cortázar, *Blow-Up and Other Stories*, pp. 67–8.
4. Cortázar, "Del cuento breve y sus alrededores," *Ultimo Round*, p. 37.
5. Cortázar, *Blow-Up and Other Stories*, p. 37.
6. Cortázar, *Blow-Up and Other Stories*, p. 24.
7. Cortázar, *Final del juego*, p. 197.
8. Cortázar, *Blow-Up and Other Stories*, p. 66.
9. Cortázar, *Blow-Up and Other Stories*, p. 56.
10. Cortázar, *Final del juego*, p. 22.
11. This story inspired Antonioni to film the movie *Blow Up*.
12. Cortázar, *Blow-Up and Other Stories*, p. 100.
13. Cortázar, *Blow-Up and Other Stories*, p. 105.
14. Cortázar, *Blow-Up and Other Stories*, p. 196.
15. Cortázar, *Cronopios and Famas*, p. 3.
16. Cortázar, *Cronopios and Famas*, p. 4.

17. Interview by Luis Mario Schneider, *Revista de la Universidad de México*, XVII, 9, May 1963, pp. 24–25.
18. L. Harss and B. Dohmann, p. 240.
19. Cortázar, *Cronopios and Famas*, p. 9.
20. André Breton, *Le Surrealisme et la peinture*, Paris, Gallimard, 1928, pp. 156–57.
21. Roger Shattuck and Simon Watson Taylor, ed., *Selected Works of Alfred Jarry*, New York, Grove Press, 1965, pp. 192–93.
22. Cortázar, *La vuelta al día en ochenta mundos*, p. 121.
23. Cortázar, *All Fires The Fire*, p. 8.
24. Cortázar, *All Fires The Fire*, p. 23.
25. Cortázar, *All Fires The Fire*, p. 29.
26. Cortázar, *All Fires The Fire*, pp. 75–76.
27. Cortázar, *The Winners*, p. 83.
28. Cortázar, *All Fires The Fire*, p. 151.
29. Cortázar, *All Fires The Fire*, p. 152.

Figures, Searches, and Centers

1. Cortázar, *The Winners*.
2. Cortázar, *The Winners*, pp. 196–97.
3. Cortázar, *Hopscotch*, p. 187.
4. Johan Huizinga, *Homo Ludens, A Study of the Play Element in Culture*, Boston, Beacon Press, 1955, p. 20.
5. Cortázar, *Hopscotch*, p. 177.
6. Cortázar, *Hopscotch*, pp. 88–9.
7. Cortázar, *Hopscotch*, p. 105.
8. Cortázar, *Hopscotch*, p. 111.
9. Cortázar, *Hopscotch*, p. 86.
10. L. Harss and B. Dohmann, pp. 229–30.
11. L. Harss and B. Dohmann, p. 231.
12. L. Harss and B. Dohmann, p. 230.
13. Cortázar, *Hopscotch*, p. 328.
14. Cortázar, *Hopscotch*, p. 49.
15. Cortázar, *Hopscotch*, pp. 163 and 166.
16. Cortázar, *Hopscotch*, pp. 76–7.

17. Cortázar, *Hopscotch*, p. 341.
18. Cortázar, *Hopscotch*, pp. 167–68.
19. Cortázar, *Hopscotch*, p. 172.
20. Cortázar, *Hopscotch*, p. 305.
21. Cortázar, *Hopscotch*, p. 334.
22. Obsessive repetitions are also a characteristic of the French "new novel" of authors such as Michel Butor and Alain Robbe-Grillet, although Cortázar has mentioned that the French "new novel" does not interest him very much.
23. Michel Butor, *Niagara*, trans. Elinor S. Miller, Chicago, Henry Regnery Company, 1969, p. 13.
24. Cortázar, *62: A Model Kit*, p. 21.
25. Cortázar, *62: A Model Kit*, pp. 273–74.
26. Cortázar, *Hopscotch*, pp. 333–34.
27. Cortázar, *Libro de Manuel*, p. 8.
28. Cortázar, *Libro de Manuel*, p. 385.

The Book As Sponge

1. Cortázar, *La vuelta al día en ochenta mundos*, p. 7.

Bibliography

1. Works by Julio Cortázar in Spanish

Presencia (Presence) by Julio Denís. Buenos Aires: Ed. El Bibliófilo, 1938.

Los reyes (The Kings). Buenos Aires: Edición de Angel Gulab, 1949. (First published in *Los anales de Buenos Aires*, Año II, no. 20, 21, 22, oct., nov., dic. 1947).

Bestiario (Bestiary). Buenos Aires: Ed. Sudamericana, 1951.

Final del juego (*End of the Game*). México: Ed. Los Presentes, 1956.

Las armas secretas (Secret Weapons). Buenos Aires: Ed. Sudamericana, 1958.

Los premios (*The Winners*). Buenos Aires: Ed. Sudamericana, 1960.

Historias de cronopios y de famas (*Cronopios and Famas*). Buenos Aires: Ed. Minotauro, 1962.

Rayuela (*Hopscotch*). Buenos Aires: Ed. Sudamericana, 1963.

Todos los fuegos el fuego (*All Fires the Fire*). Buenos Aires: Ed. Sudamericana, 1966.

La vuelta al día en ochenta mundos (Around the Day in Eighty Worlds). México: Ed. Siglo Veintiuno, 1967.

62: Modelo para armar (*62: A Model Kit*). Buenos Aires, Ed. Sudamericana, 1968.

Buenos Aires Buenos Aires. Fotografías de Alicia D'Amico y Sara Facio. Buenos Aires: Ed. Sudamericana, 1968.

Ultimo Round (Last Round). México: Ed. Siglo Veintiuno, 1969.

Viaje alrededor de una mesa (*Trip Around a Table*). Buenos Aires: Ed. Rayuela, 1970.

Pameos y meopas (Pameos and Meopas). Barcelona: OCNOS, Editorial Libre de Sinera, 1971.

Prosa del observatorio (Prose from the Observatory). Barcelona: Ed. Lumen, 1972.

Libro de Manuel (Book of Manuel). Buenos Aires: Ed. Sudamericana, 1973.

2. *Works by Julio Cortázar Translated into English*

End of the Game and Other Stories, including stories from *Bestiary*, *Secret Weapons*, and *End of the Game.* Translated by Paul Blackburn. New York: Pantheon, 1963.

The Winners. Translated by Elaine Kerrigan. New York: Pantheon, 1965.

Hopscotch. Translated by Gregory Rabassa. New York: Pantheon, 1966.

Blow Up and Other Stories, a reprinted version of *End of the Game and Other Stories.* New York: Pantheon, 1967.

Cronopios and Famas. Translated by Paul Blackburn. New York: Pantheon, 1969.

62: A Model Kit. Translated by Gregory Rabassa. New York: Pantheon, 1972.

All Fires the Fire. Translated by Suzanne Jill Levine. New York: Pantheon, 1973.

3. *Works Translated by Julio Cortázar into Spanish*

Daniel Defoe. *Robinson Crusoe.* Viau.

Walter de la Mare. *Memorias de una enana.* Argos.

G. K. Chesterton. *El hombre que sabía demasiado.* Nova.
Andre Gide. *El inmoralista.* Argos.
Lord Houghton. *Vida y cartas de John Keats.* Iman.
Alfred Stern. *La filosofía existencial de Jean-Paul Sartre.* Iman.
Alfred Stern. *Filosofía de la risa y del llanto.* Iman.
Jean Giono. *Nacimiento de la Odisea.* Argos.
Edgar Allan Poe. *Obras en prosa.* Trad. y Notas. Universidad de Puerto Rico.
Margueritte Yourcenar. *Memorias de Adriano.* Ed. Sudamericana.

4. *Articles, Reviews, Essays by Julio Cortázar (a partial listing)*

"Rimbaud." Julio Denís. *Huella 2*, Buenos Aires, (1941).
"La urna griega en la poesía de Keats." *Revista de Estudios Clásicos*, II, Mendoza, (1946).
"Notas sobre lo novela contemporanea." *Realidad* 8, Buenos Aires, (1948), 240–46.
"Muerte de Antonin Artaud." *Sur* 163, Buenos Aires, mayo 1948, 80–82.
"Graham Greene: *The Heart of the Matter.*" *Realidad* 13, Buenos Aires, febrero 1949, 107–12.
"Leopoldo Marechal: *Adan Buenosayres.*" *Realidad* 14, marzo–abril, 1949, 232–38.
"Un cadaver viviente." *Realidad* 15, mayo–junio 1949, 349–50.
"Irracionalismo y eficacia." *Realidad* 17–18, sept.–dic. 1949, 250–59.
"Francois Porche: Baudelaire, historia de un alma." *Sur* 176, junio 1949, 70–74.
"Octavio Paz: *Libertad bajo palabra.*" *Sur* 182, dic. 1949, 93–95.
"Cyril Connolly: La tumba sin sosiego." *Sur* 184, feb. 1950, 61–63.
"Victoria Ocampo: *Soledad sonora.*" *Sur* 192–94, oct.–dic. 1950, 294–97.

"Situación de la novela." *Cuadernos Americanos*, vol. LII, 4, México, julio–agosto 1950, 223–43.
"Los olvidados." *Sur* 209–210, marzo–abril 1952, 170–72.
"Gardel." *Sur* 223, julio–agosto, 1953, 127–29.
"Para una poética." *La Torre 7*, Puerto Rico, 1952, 121–38.
"Algunos aspectos del cuento." *Revista Casa de las Américas* 15–16, Habana 1962–63, 3–14.
"Julio Cortázar al 'Che'." *La estafeta literaria* 383, Madrid, 18 nov. 1967, 9.
"Carta a Roberto Fernández Retamar." *Casa de las Américas* 45, dic. 1967, 5–12.
"Saludos de Julio Cortázar." *Life en español*, vol. 33, no. 7, 1969.

5. *Works about Julio Cortázar*

Amicola, José. *Sobre Cortázar.* Argentina: Ed. Escuela, 1969.
Barrenechea, Ana María. "*Rayuela*, una busqueda a partir de cero." *Sur*, No. 288 (1964), pp. 69–73.
Curutchet, Juan Carlos. *Julio Cortázar o la crítica de la razón pragmática.* Madrid: Ed. Nacional, 1972.
De Sola, Graciela. *Julio Cortázar y el hombre nuevo.* Buenos Aires, Ed. Sudamericana, 1968.
De Tirri, Sara Vinocur and Tirri, Nestor. *La vuelta a Cortázar en nueve ensayos.* Buenos Aires, Carlos Pérez, 1968.
Figueroa Amaral, Esperanza. "Guía para el lector de *Rayuela*." *Revista Iberoamericana* XXXII (1966), pp. 261–66.
García Canclini, Néstor. *Cortázar, una antropologia poetica.* Buenos Aires: Ed. Nova, 1968.
Garfield, Evelyn Picon. *¿Es Julio Cortázar un surrealista?* Madrid: Ed. Gredos, to be released in 1974.
——————. "The Exquisite Cadaver of Surrealism." *Review* 72, Winter (1972), pp. 18–21. This *Review* has many articles about Cortázar in English.

Giacoman, Helmy, ed. *Homenaje a Julio Cortázar.* New York: Las Américas, 1972.

Gonzalez Bermejo, Ernesto. "Una apuesta a lo imposible." In *Cosas de escritores.* Montevideo: Marcha, 1971, pp. 91–136.

Guibert, Rita. "Julio Cortázar." In *Seven Voices.* New York: Alfred A. Knopf, 1972, pp. 277–302.

Harss, Luis and Dohmann, Barbara. "Julio Cortázar, or the Slap in the Face." In *Into the Mainstream.* New York: Harper and Row, 1966, pp. 206–245. (*Los nuestros.* Buenos Aires: Ed. Sudamericana, 1966.)

Irby, James E. "Cortázar's *Hopscotch and Other Games.*" In *Novel—Forum on Fiction.* Vol. I, No. 1, pp. 64–70.

MacAdam, Alfred J. "The Individual and the Other: A Study of the Prose Works of Julio Cortázar," Dissertation, Princeton (1969). (*El indivíduo y el otro.* Buenos Aires: Ed. La Librería, 1971.)

Morello-Frosch, Marta. "Julio Cortázar: From Beasts to Bolts." *Books Abroad.* Vol. 44, No. 1 (Winter 1970), pp. 22–25.

Schneider, Luis Mario. "Entrevista con Julio Cortázar." *Revista de la Universidad de México.* Vol. XVII, No. 9 (1963), pp. 24–25.

Simo, Ana María. *Cinco mirades sobre Cortázar.* Buenos Aires: Ed. Tiempo Contemporáneo, 1968.

Index